# The Study of Education:
# An Introduction

**Also available from Continuum**

*Comparative and International Education*, David Philips,
   Michele Schweisfurth and Erwin Epstein

*Exploring Key Issues in Education*, Dean Garrett and Derek Kassem

*An Introduction to Assessment*, Patricia Broadfoot

*An Introduction to Education Studies*, Sue Warren

*Key Issues in Secondary Education*, John Beck and Mary Earl

*Philosophy of Education*, Richard Pring

*Psychology and the Teacher 8th Edition*, Dennis Child

*A Sociology of Educating 5th Edition*, Roland Meighan, Clive Harber, Len Barton,
   Iram Siraj-Blatchford and Stephen Walker

# The Study of Education: An Introduction

**Jane Bates and Sue Lewis**

continuum

Continuum International Publishing Group
The Tower Building          80 Maiden Lane
11 York Road                Suite 704
London SE1 7NX              New York, NY 10038

www.continuumbooks.com

**British Library Cataloguing-in-Publication Data**
A catalogue record for this book is available from the British Library.

ISBN: 978-08264-9976-9 (paperback)
      978-14411-2861-4 (hardback)

**Library of Congress Cataloging-in-Publication Data**
Bates, Jane.
Ths Study of education: an introduction / Jane Bates and Sue Lewis.
    p. cm.   Includes bibliographical references and index.
  ISBN 978-1-4411-2861-4 (hardback)
  ISBN 978-0-8264-9976-9 (pbk.)
1. Education–Philosophy. 2. Education–Aims and objectives. 3. Education–
Study and teaching. I. Lewis, Sue. II. Title.

LB14.7.B38 2009
370–dc22

                                        2008045239

Typeset by Newgen Imaging Systems Pvt Ltd, Chennai, India
Printed and bound in Great Britain by Athenaeum Press Ltd., Gateshead, Tyne & Wear

# Contents

# Acknowledgements

Our thanks to

Dave Dickinson, Wendy Whittaker and our students for their autobiographies.

Lois Gyves and Alison Sheldon from PfS, J. G. Ashley from RMCH and Laura Bryce from Salford Foundation.

Suzanne Spicer, Yukiko Davenne and Derek Wolland.

Andrew, successfully teaching in Dublin.

And most of all, to Trevor and Albert for their patience throughout the 'summer that never was'.

# Part One
## Personal Journeys

# Writing the Self: Educational Autobiography

**1**

## Chapter Outline

## Stories and oral histories

How do we find out what school was like in the past? How do we know what people learnt and what kind of values education eschewed? In addition to the traditional history of schools and schooling as recorded in official documents and by academics, there are the more personal accounts of schooldays, both fictional and non-fictional, recorded by ordinary people, that provide us with a window to the past. For example, there are the numerous 'stories' about schools and schooling that appear in literature such as *Tom Brown's Schooldays* (1857) by Thomas Hughes and the more contemporary *Tom Kipper's Schooldays: Memories of an Irish Childhood* (2007) by Peter Sale; in films such as *To Sir With Love* (1967) based on the novel by E. R. Braithwaite and *The Prime of Miss Jean Brodie* (1969) based on the book by Muriel Spark (1961); and also on television, for example in *Teachers* (Channel Four 2001–2005) and Grange Hill (BBC 1978–2008). Some of these are stories of formal education, others are more personal accounts of learning experiences, of relationships with friends and teachers and of learning in different contexts (Brunner 1994: 12). Brunner (1994) suggests that such texts provide the reader with 'useful explorations' of a variety of themes, including the relationship between teachers and pupils, issues of class, race and gender and the hidden curriculum (ibid.: 12).

Personal oral accounts of schooldays provide a similar window to the past. According to Brown (1988), the oral recounting of 'stories' has always been the main way in which non-literate societies have preserved and passed on their collective knowledge and cultural understandings. She points to the fact that in some tribes in West Africa, a specific member of the tribe – the 'griot' – is the person who is tasked with 'remembering' these 'stories', which often intertwine fictional aspects with historical and cultural understandings to aid the storytelling process (Brown 1988: 3).

In the Western world, however, oral traditions have been replaced by written accounts. Such written accounts of history have, however, usually been provided from the perspective of a dominant male elite and have, thus, generally excluded the stories of ordinary people, in particular, women, that are often preserved by a more oral tradition. The development of tape recording and later digital sound and video recording has revolutionized the collection of oral histories, and has led to a recognition of the value of recording the views and life stories of ordinary people. Van Oteghen suggests that in education, the use of oral histories can enable students to 'more fully appreciate the present once they realize how people confronted difficulties of earlier times' (1996: 45).

---

### Activity 1.1

Compare your own experiences of school and schooling with those portrayed in a variety of literary sources, in films and in television programmes.

Interview an older relative or acquaintance in the 70 plus age group. Try to find out about their early childhood experiences, their schooling, their family life, work and career and their view of life-long learning. Again, compare their experiences and views on education with your own.

Visit the Edwardians Online Website, an online archive of oral histories relating to work and family life in the period prior to 1918. The archive can be found at: www.qualidata.ac.uk/edwardians/search/Yj_themeExa.asp?id=11

You will find a number of selected oral histories on the website that will enable you to compare the educational experiences of individuals from a variety of social backgrounds.

---

# Educational autobiographies

*A life lived is what actually happens. A life as experienced consists of the images, feelings, sentiments, desires, thoughts and meanings known to the person whose life it is . . . a life as told, a life history is a narrative influenced by the cultural conversations of telling, by the audience and by the social context.*

*(Bruner 1984: 7 in Usher 1998: 18)*

According to Karpiak (2000), autobiographical writing arose as a narrative form at the end of the eighteenth century. Its origins lie in the writing of personal 'memoirs' and religious confessions. Whilst the latter writings focused on personal transgressions and sins, auto-biographical writings produced a more holistic view of the self, what Haworth (1980 in Karpaik 2000: 33) termed a 'self portrait', based on self analysis and self understanding. According to Schrader (2004) a number of terms such as biography, life story, autobiography and narrative all refer to a written account of an individual's life, whilst an *educational autobiography* is a written life story that focuses explicitly on an individual's learning experiences. The difference between the oral histories that we considered earlier and an educational autobiography is that:

> . . . in oral history the aim is to gain information about the past . . . (in autobiography), to grasp the ways in which a particular person constructs and makes sense of his or her life at a given moment. (Plummer 1983: 105 in Ribbens 1993: 87)

In the past, autobiographical writing was mainly a male domain, and generally pro-gressed as a linear narrative in which a notion of self identity progressively emerged. Kehily suggests that such writings generally portrayed a peculiarly 'professional male experience as the sum total of human experience . . . free of ambiguity and contradiction, shaped for and by the public domain' (1995: 29). More contemporary writings by previously marginalized groups in society, such as women and homosexuals, have challenged this traditional form and allowed for more varied explorations of identity (ibid.). This leads us to Jackson's (1990) notion of 'critical autobiography', in which identity and views of self are considered to be 'fluid and fragmented' and influenced by both social context and audience (ibid.: 30–31).

Autobiography, therefore, as a method seeks to capture 'the unity of the self and the situation' (Pinar 1981 in O'Brien and Schillaci 2002: 28). According to Ribbens, autobiographical enquiry enables individuals to consider the links between everyday experiences, such as schooling and 'institutionalized knowledge', or more precisely, to consider the links between their 'private understanding' and the more 'public' ways of understanding and knowing (1993: 83).

In the post-modern era, therefore, an acceptance has developed for the use of narrative and autobiography as a vehicle for exploring reality. Creating our own stories as text is the ultimate in asserting and redefining our identity. Out of this comes the use of 'a personal cultural reflection' (Curtis 1998: 28). Through telling our 'stories', we can subjectify our experience and communicate our own reality to others. This gives us an opportunity to explore different perspectives that have influenced our lives, in particular, those that have shaped our educational experience. It is also important to try and set our experience in a broader context in order to understand how the microcosm relates to the macrocosm. In this way, we begin to discover the shared aspects of our lives that others can recognize, or have, in fact, experienced themselves. Also, it helps us to make sense of our lives within the context of the bigger social picture.

> . . . it is through the telling of stories that people make sense of their lives . . . the power of stories (is that) they can create connections that enhance learning, and they can give meaning to our

unique lived experience . . . After all, stories are lived before they are told. (MacIntyre cited in Jalongo and Isenberg 1995 in O'Brien and Schillaci 2002: 27)

# Personal journeys

The writing of an autobiography can be a cathartic process that enables us to make sense of our disjointed experiences and decipher patterns. Thus, whatever our social or ethnic background, we can, as a consequence of 'writing ourselves', achieve a deepened sense of self. As bell hooks (1989) explains, we all have a 'need' to disseminate material about our particular experience (in Curtis 1998).

The writing of an autobiography can thus promote self-reflection and help us to both dissect and to reconstruct our identity and in so doing, to better understand the identity of others. The use of autobiography is, therefore, particularly important for those who are to become teachers, or other professionals working with children. We, therefore, use autobiography with first year students on our Education Studies programme in order to encourage them to begin to make sense of their own stories in the light of educational policy and processes. As Rousmaniere suggests:

> This semi structured writing exercise gives students the opportunity to understand personally how their own education developed through a combination of their own individual life circumstances, personality, and family, with dominant social conditions of their gender, race and class. In the process of this reflection, students come to view more clearly how education 'happens' in this society and what really matters to children in schools. It is an educational exercise based on personal introspection, but it is also deeply rooted in the understanding of schooling as a social and political phenomenon. (Rousmaniere 2000: 88)

There are of course criticisms levelled at the use of autobiography. Some suggest that it is rather self indulgent and overly subjective. As an approach, particularly in research, autobiography, like oral history, is often viewed as being open to fabrication, inaccurate memories and concealment of events and facts (Ingram 1979 in Ribbens 1993). Ribbens also points to the issues associated with 'how a public audience can know about private matters' (1993: 87).

In addition to the criticisms about the approach, there are a number of ethical issues that surround autobiographical writing, particularly when it is used for assessment purposes. Monteagudo (2005: 12) highlights the following ethical concerns:

- there should be no obligation, nor any negative consequences for the student
- all information revealed by the author is confidential, and any information that contains specific reference to others, for example family members, should only be made with those individuals prior consent and approval
- no defamatory or derogatory comments should be made

Some researchers, like Maylor, also suggest that autobiography 'can be a very painful and traumatic experience', pointing to the fact that Lewis (1992: 5) questions the validity of autobiography as an educational activity, suggesting that it is more 'a form of pedagogic terrorism' (Maylor 1995: 39).

Before you start writing your own educational autobiography, it is possibly useful to stop and consider how other people have approached such a project. The following excerpts are taken from the autobiographies of our students and also the educators whose life histories are used to inform our course. Their stories represent the general progression that normally takes place in such writings, from those of the student, starting to explore their emerging identity and experience in terms of class, race and gender, through to the mature educator, who adds to those initial reflections the relationship between personal experiences and the development of approaches to pedagogy and eventually the contextualization of experience with respect to politics, policy and professional practice.

## Student S

In one student's account of her early experiences of school, it is ethnic origin that is a significant factor in shaping her memories. *Student S*, as we shall call her, has realized:

> The power of the primary school teacher is such that she can make you extremely happy and confident or extremely humiliated and powerless in front of her and her class.

Teachers, as well as pupils, should acknowledge that we are all racialized and gendered beings, products of our social background, and that we all are capable of recognizing where and when we fit in. Indeed, as Curtis (1998) maintains, teachers need to recognize that they are part of the context of the classroom and, as such, have an enormous influence on children's learning and self-esteem. *Student S* continues:

> It was predominantly white, middle-class, in fact, in my first year there were only five Asian girls in the whole school. Consequently, we stood out, and not in a way that evoked positive responses. I dressed differently, looked different and had a whole different lifestyle to my classmates. Consequently, I became very introvert, reserved, shy and extremely self-conscious. There was always the sense that we were looked down upon by others, we stood out yet were still considered part of the wallpaper. Academically, the Asian girls were extremely strong, but this was not of any importance. Our achievements had no value.

Here, *Student S* was learning the harsh lesson that some people's success is worth more than others' in terms of their cultural capital and that, for some pupils, school becomes a context in which they have to try and reconcile multiple identities; sometimes, as Reay (2004) comments, aspiring to the norms of the school may demand a betrayal of who they are. Thus, *Student S* was later, temporarily, excluded from school for daring to suggest that money spent on space exploration might be better spent in supporting developing countries, although, ironically, she believed that were she to appear to reject her cultural values, teachers would have supported her 'brave' stance as a rebel.

This is an extreme example of the self denial the school seemed to demand, 'we had no names and were often referred to as the Asian girls,' an overt case of being forced to lose one's identity as a trade-off for being accepted. This echoes Reay's (2004) case study where she explores the experiences of widening participation students in Higher Education. Reay (2004) suggests that such students face a dilemma of whether they have to leave behind their working class identity in order to adopt the identity of the 'achieving student'. *Student S* has certainly understood early in life the message from the school that, as she is, she has little social value.

> I can say with conviction that our identity as Muslims made it far worse for us, had we rebelled against our own religion we would have appeared more acceptable to both teachers and students. Then the teachers would have said we were free, or that we had exercised our basic freedom of speech by disowning our religion. Only freedom of speech that has been given the stamp of approval is acceptable, what a double edged paradox.

What is more, the imputed identity ascribed by the school was 'Asian' and that was the label that governed the school's response to her, not the fact that, materially, her family were, in fact, middle class. Here we can see the force of institutional racism at work (see Chapter 6). Ultimately, as with many of those who do not fit the dominant culture, *Student S* learned the rules and played the game. 'I needed the education system to get somewhere, despite hating it.'

## Student T

Another first year student, *Student T*, has also started the process of evaluating her own educational experience through questioning the notion of relative cultural capital (see Garratt and Pickard 2007) and challenging accepted hierarchies in that regard.

> My own educational experience has been fraught with battles of epic and not so epic proportions; those that have involved local education authorities, schools, fellow students and myself. Most people would try to forget what pain education has caused them, but recently through evaluation of the events of my educational story and those who helped me along the way, I realised that by confronting it I may be able to use my experiences to help others.

*Student T*'s early experience of learning was positive, being situated within a strong family context:

> My parents encouraged inquisitiveness and instilled that as long as we worked hard we would receive what we deserved; society had other ideas.

Fortunately, she recognizes quite clearly that early lessons from parents would provide a secure framework in which to locate further experience:

> The first school I attended . . . I remember being truly happy there as they promoted autonomy in learning and the idea that if a child is able to do something . . . they nurtured the interest. By the

time I was forced to leave at 5, my reading abilities had increased dramatically, my mum would have to get me books from Central Library because I had read the entire collection at school. I was not overtly resistant to the schooling process from then on, but as the years went by and I was denied opportunity after opportunity, I realised that I was never going to get the same education as someone living in a wealthier area . . . It was sad but at such an early age my innocence in regards to education was lost and although I knew I was different because I was black, that was something I could not change – in my eyes my parents worked harder than the people with money I came across . . . yet their tax bracket was defining what education I was entitled to.

After six months in secondary school, *Student T* noticed that she was being treated differently:

. . . it occurred to me that it was because I was labelled as disruptive. My friend SB, who had ADHD, and I were the first to be blamed if something went missing or a situation arose, consequently we conformed to their ideas of us – if they expected us to misbehave we did, and they could do nothing to us because we did very well in our tests and examinations.

Some time later, *Student T* was accepted to the National Academy for Gifted and Talented Youth, yet despite receiving guidance on appropriate teaching methods, teachers at her school were unable to deal with her, and she defied the label.

I did not fit in with the stereotype portrayed by the black pupils. I spent about 40 per cent of the first three years and 20 per cent of the last two years excluded from school.

*Student T* is able to relate her personal experience to the literature that consequently enhances her own expression, thus she suggests that:

It is noted by Klein (2000: 9) that exclusion from school means being on the outside, alienated from the mainstream . . . It means being branded as a problem and carrying that problematic identity around with you, possibly for the rest of your life. By branding me as such in primary school, wherever I went I was dealt with as though I were a time bomb about to explode.

However, *Student T* does acknowledge the importance of the help she received from those teachers who made her feel 'valued' and goes on to quote Bartlett and Burton (2007: 11) that:

. . . personal resonances of the term 'education' are shaped by a number of individual experiences such as coming top of the class . . . being made fun of by pupils or teachers.

She continues:

This was my experience and Klein (2000: 14) describes it as being a 'square peg being pushed through a round hole', then after a while they have no time to try and make you fit so go back to those who are round and fit easily.

Finally, the school put together a programme of home, independent and school study, which provided a beneficial learning experience, yet, as with *Student S* earlier, she acknowledges that academic success comes at a price:

> By choosing to resist the dominant model I was targeted as a sell-out, because there was a perception that successful black people have given up their culture – in my eyes my culture was the wisdom and pride my parents had instilled within me rather than a way of dressing, speaking or behaving.

*Student T* is able to manifest a sophisticated understanding of the complex nature of identity that young people have to negotiate during their journey through the school system. We have used the process of autobiography with students, therefore, as a means of recognizing the value of such 'accumulated assets of young people, brought from their communities to the process of formal education' (Garratt and Pickard 2007: 6). This allows us to challenge 'manifestations of dissonance between the knowledge, skills and abilities of dominant groups in society and alternative forms of cultural wealth' (ibid.).

## Wendy

Wendy's exploration of her earlier educational life through autobiography has helped her to understand her current professional style and philosophy, which, in turn, has enabled her to be a more effective teacher. Wendy interprets her experience very much from the perspective of her role as a specialist in early years education, particularly in relation to teaching and learning styles. For example:

> The headteacher of my infants school was a sour, unemotional middle-aged woman. As a secret survival mechanism, all pupils aged under seven knew the 'anti-head' conspiratorial school chant that somehow helped us to believe that she was not all-powerful and all-knowing. As an adult I now recognise that aside from the personality traits that rigidly dis-endeared us to her, it was her teaching style and approach that most made me fearful and lacking in confidence. She embodied Locke's empirical pedagogical approach that knowledge had to be transmitted to the child who was a 'tabula rasa' (1690) – a 'blank slate' waiting to be instructed and taught in the ways of the world, rejecting any notions of intrinsic motivation in learning. I loathed her for her remoteness, and retreated into myself whenever she taught a lesson in our class; 'only a child with an exceptionally confident learning stance is likely to take any chances within a context in which risks and costs of failure are high'. (Pollard 1996: 11)

Wendy goes on to contrast her early experience of the English system with those in an elementary school in upstate New York:

> Classes were taught in a relaxed, open environment, with a greater emphasis on fluid and group learning than that modelled by my previous infants school in its empiricist approach. It was a pedagogic style I was not accustomed to, and reflect now that the insecurity I felt about the cultural

change was what Piaget termed 'disequilibration' (1985). I had to assimilate a new pedagogy and accommodate to it. (Boden 1994: 6)

This was a far more relaxed school, with an emphasis on group learning, yet Wendy's memory is focused on the insecurity she felt when faced with 'having to assimilate a new pedagogy'. Had she remained in that environment, it is possible that she would have continued to engage with the education system. However, after returning to the UK, Wendy found herself increasingly disengaged with learning:

. . . (I) engaged less and less with the didactic and emotionally distant learning that took place. Had I known of Friedrich Froebel at that age, I would have agreed with his view that to be engaged involves 'spirit, intellect, volition and emotions' (Lilley 1967: 8). It was not until later in my life that I realised that my own lack of enthusiasm for school education was not a product of a deficient brain, but more likely a lack of engagement in the learning process.

Much later, during her degree programme, Wendy finally found a learning process that did enable her to create her own meanings:

After my 'A' levels, I completed a Joint Honours degree in Creative Arts, which I absolutely loved because I engaged with the subject, and was able to 'construct' (Piaget 1985) my own meanings and learning – this was the first time I had experienced feeling like a 'fish in water' (Laevers 1994: 15). I now believe that for many adults, Higher Education may be the first opportunity they have had to experience a constructivist pedagogy, where their own learning is not solely predicated on the knowledge and transmission abilities of the teacher: 'within a constructivist pedagogy, the teacher seriously considers what the child brings to the learning situation as well as what he or she wishes to transmit'. (Athey 1994: 31)

This has resonance with Reay's (2004) comments on the experiences of other adult learners who find that, as adults, they are able to engage with education in a successful way for the first time in their lives. Wendy also refers to the work of Knowles (1984) who coined the phrase 'andragogy' to differentiate the learning characteristics of adults and children. She argues that Reay, however, would suggest that for some adults of working class origin, and for minority ethnic students, the process of succeeding in higher education does not come without its sacrifices and challenges.

Wendy also finds herself in sympathy with some of the radical educational philosophers we will consider in Chapter 7, in that her own teaching style is based on the notion of 'practice reflexivity'. She has come to believe that academics need to be continually reflecting critically on their own teaching and actively pursuing their own learning. She also sees herself as a facilitator whose role is to encourage the natural seeking spirit of the learner, whatever their age.

I still feel that I am in the process of experimentation – trying, testing and thinking about how I teach. My heartfelt desire is that students experience deep-level learning where they enter their 'zone of proximal development' (Vygotsky 1978) and experience what Csiksentmihalyi (1990) calls 'being in a state of flow'. My experiences have taught me that the relationship between learner and teacher is critical. To fully engage the learner in the process, the teacher has to encourage the natural activity and inquisition of the learner – whether they be adult or child.

While Wendy's autobiography was focused on an examination of her experiences as both a learner and a teacher, the following autobiographical account demonstrates a greater integration of personal experience and the wider social and political context.

## My educational autobiography

### By David Dickinson

In the summer of 1960 in a small village near Newark-on-Trent, Nottinghamshire one third of the 10 and 11 year olds were wearing their new grammar school uniforms and looking forward to new, or in my case second-hand, bicycles as a reward for passing the 11+. My brother didn't pass the 11+ and so didn't get a uniform and didn't get a bicycle. By the time my youngest brother was of secondary age, all the schools in the area had become comprehensive. Seven years followed in my single sex, rugby playing grammar school where I gained seven O levels, four A levels and rugby colours, prizes for outstanding work and industry, and RE. But it wasn't until near the end of the sixth form period that I was encouraged by my form teacher to apply for university, one of those faraway places that seemed to be only for rich, *posh* people who could speak better than me and had more confidence. He explained how to apply. I didn't know because no one else in my immediate or distant family had ever been to university. It wasn't for us, we believed.

At the grammar school, apart from a few caring individuals, the teaching was mainly by fear and my achievements were a product of my desire to find out as much as I could, especially about History, French and Literature. I didn't exactly endear myself to the grammar school staff when I wrote an article for the school magazine entitled *Comprehensive Schools: A Social Necessity*. My parents would have performed well in comprehensive school, but were denied that right. Although they had a basic education, like many others prior to 1945, my parents were denied the right to ask and learn about everything under the stars and beyond.

My original aim, after obtaining a degree in History and Politics at the University of Kent at Canterbury, was to seek a qualification so I could work abroad. This took me on a one year PGCE course at the University of Lancaster to train in the teaching of History and Humanities. My first teaching practice was at a Catholic Comprehensive School in Lancashire, and following this practice I was asked to write about the essential characteristics of an effective teacher. I sardonically wrote:

> All the teachers in my teaching practice school believed, or rather kidded themselves, that in their own ways they were effective teachers. Some were blatantly ineffective but many, at a superficial glance, appeared to be effective. A deeper glare showed the flimsiness of their effectiveness. The apparently effective ones marched into a classroom stern-faced and looking ready for action, ready that is, to awe the class into submission. The teacher talks for ten minutes or so while the children are ordered to listen on pain of being sent out or 'clobbered'. After the teacher has finished speaking, the children put their heads down and write something in their books, ready for finishing at home. This has supposedly been effective teaching because the children have apparently listened, done some written work (useful for end of year exam), and, above all, behaved. Essential characteristics necessary for this kind

of effective teaching are inflexibility, a loud voice, large hands, a dominant, extrovert personality, the ability to be bitingly sarcastic, a quick wit, knowledge of different methods of torture and a capacity to indulge in self-delusion.

These teachers' styles in general mirrored that of my grammar school teachers. Are there still people who claim these were the good old days of education when standards were much higher?

But things were beginning to change. Harold Wilson's Labour government had introduced comprehensive schools in the '60s, and the '70s began with John Lennon's *Imagine* topping the charts, *'imagine all the people sharing all the world'*. Alternative, radical schools were set up. One of my bibles was Neil Portman and Charles Weingartner's *Teaching As a Subversive Activity* (1969), in which they rejected the *vaccination* theory of education:

> English is not history and history is not science and science is not art and art is not music and minor subjects and English, history and science major subjects, and a subject is something you 'take' and, when you have taken it, you have 'had' it, and if you have 'had' it you are immune and need not take it again.

It is fascinating how in 2008 this *vaccination* theory of education is being rejected again in favour of skills-based, cross curricular approaches.

I was appointed to my first post, to teach History and Humanities, at an 11–18 Community Comprehensive School on a tough new housing estate in Liverpool. As well as an innovative teacher-designed CSE course, there was an opportunity to develop integrated approaches to teaching across subjects in a school that had an Adult Education Officer, parents in lessons, and was at the heart of its local community. In fact it was just what is being advocated today in the new Children's Plan. After five exciting years I wanted to continue teaching in this country and was promoted in 1977 to the post of Head of Humanities at a 13–16 school in Rochdale, where I had the opportunity to develop a CSE Humanities course and link it to the development of a teacher-designed O level course predating the introduction of GCSEs. As Chief Moderator and Chief Examiner, I was able to play a pivotal role throughout the '80s in developing GCSE integrated courses. There followed a one year secondment first to obtain an M. Ed. in anti-racist Education, and then a two year secondment as an Equal Opportunities Officer working across Tameside and Rochdale Local Education Authorities (LEAs).

Another bible of mine was *The Challenge for the Comprehensive School*, written by David Hargreaves in 1982. He wrote:

> An increasing number of pupils will continue to be prepared for higher education, but we must also prepare pupils for the new elite positions, such as trade union officials, local councillors and community leaders. We need men and women who will take greater responsibility for the vitality of the various committees, including the local residential committees of which they will become members. These committees need to be more self-determining, more self-reliant and more democratically controlled. It is on that basis that a stronger national solidarity can be founded. We must all improve our skills in the resolution of conflict among the nation's sub-committees.

By now the Conservatives were running the country, and following some social upheaval, including race riots in various cities at the beginning of the '80s, they were keen to develop the *national solidarity,* spoken of by David Hargreaves, through recognition in schools of pressing race and gender issues, and through the introduction of a more prescribed National Curriculum.

After ten years in Greater Manchester with the delights and challenges of a variety of roles reflecting national developments, I moved to Gateshead to take up a two year Fixed Term Headship at an 11–16 mixed comprehensive school from 1988–90. After ten years of Thatcherism, the market economy was also embracing education and much to my amusement, I found myself in the Daily Mail because of the school's new prospectus, marketing approaches and links with local businesses. After this two year apprenticeship, I was successful in obtaining my second Headship at a high-performing comprehensive school in Winchester, Hampshire, the Henry Beaufort School. High-performing? Well this wasn't surprising given that at least 70 per cent of the parents in the area had attended higher education themselves and most (although many had the finance) decided to use the local state comprehensive rather than opting for private schools. This meant it had a true comprehensive intake. My ten year experience at this school showed me how high aspirations help achievement, but it was *achievement with care,* the school's motto.

National Ofsted inspections were introduced in the '90s, and with it much more accountability. SATs were also brought in. But alongside this came less local control of schools by the direct financing of those that wished to become grant maintained. The headteacher's role was changing from leading teachers to more that of a Chief Executive, Chief Networker, Chief Bidder. Specialist schools were introduced offering the promise of an extra £200,000 per year if a successful bid was made, bids based on data targets. League tables were introduced making school more accountable.

I believe that after ten years in a school, it's hard to constantly reinvent yourself as a headteacher and so, rather than quietly running down, at the age of 50 I sought a new challenge further north in the type of inner city environment that I had taught in prior to 1990. I was successfully appointed Head of Haywood, an 11–16 comprehensive, similar in size with just over 1000 students, to the school I had left in Hampshire. It wasn't a school that needed a fresh start nor had it been anywhere near special measures, but is in one of the most deprived areas in the country, in one of the most deprived cities. Over the past eight years I have been able to develop the school at the heart of the local community, as a fully extended school with a specialism in Engineering, successfully bid to host a City Learning Centre through the government's 'Excellence in Cities' money and establish it as a core/change school for Creative Partnerships, working on the development of the Student Voice and exciting curriculum innovation.

Described by Osfted inspectors in May 2007 as 'a special place, a good school with outstanding features, with outstanding care, support and guidance', the school is well placed to develop its educational vision as a restructured school of the future, if it is allowed to. Well, the last few years have been turbulent. The government has promised to revamp or rebuild all schools. Tony Blair was elected in 1997 with the mantra 'education, education, education', and backed this up with money especially for inner city areas. But should the government's programme 'Building Schools for the Future' be renamed 'Closing Schools for the Future'? The development of Sure Start centres, speaking classes, reduction of poverty, will ultimately have an effect, so that children will no longer enter secondary school 'well below average'.

What will not work is threatening schools, linking them with closure or being independent, privately financed academies because not enough children are obtaining higher grades including English and Maths. My Liverpool, Rochdale and Gateshead schools would have been closed because they did not meet the criteria. At Haywood, we have fought off the threat of closure. My Winchester school did not and doesn't face any threat at all. It's interesting to compare the two schools. Both have recently been described by Ofsted as 'good with outstanding features', and the gap in performance with one school obtaining 55 per cent higher grades, including English and Maths, and the other 31 per cent only reflects the area they are in.

ICT-dominated schools of the future will be radically different, but the quality of teaching and learning and the quality of relationships should continue to be regarded as very important. Increasingly, the only people who will be educated will be those who have learned to learn, the people who have learned how to adapt and change, the people who have realized no knowledge is secure. The Principal of an American High School hands this letter to new teachers when they start at his school:

> Dear Teacher,
>
> I am a survivor of a concentration camp. My eyes saw what no man should witness: gas chambers built by learned engineers, children poisoned by educated physicians, infants killed by trained nurses, women and babies shot and burned by high school and college graduates. So I am suspicious of education.
>
> My request is: Help your students become human. Your effects must never produce learned monsters, skilled psychopaths, educated Eichmans.
>
> Reading, writing, arithmetic are important only if they serve to make our children more human. (In Ord 2006)

This has been pinned up in every school that I have worked in. Will this message be on the screens of our schools of the future?

*David Dickinson is the Headteacher of Haywood Engineering College, Stoke on Trent*

## Activity 1.2

In writing his educational autobiography, what has been the defining feature of David Dickinson's identity that has informed his experience?

Can you identify any particular perspectives, ideological or philosophical, that have informed his practice as an educator and role as a headteacher?

# Writing 'your self'

*Our early experiences of education should shape our adult ways of evaluating schooling. What really did matter to our childhood selves in those early experiences of schooling? What worked or didn't work, what furthered our sense of ability and progress in schooling? What made us want to come to school, what made us want to run away? What are the social and structural conditions that made our experiences differ – what were the economic, racial, ethnic and gendered variables that combine so that I ran happily to school (almost) every morning while others found schooling extraneous to their life, burdensome, painful, humiliating, or simply boring?*

*(Rousmaniere 2000: 88)*

Writing an educational autobiography is not just about recalling our experiences of schooling, but an act of self reflection that seeks to enable us to understand how our unique experiences were shaped by our social class, gender, race, ability, family, politics and our relationships with our peers and teachers and more (Rousmaniere 2000). The major benefit of writing an educational autobiography, according to Schrader, is therefore 'not what you can learn about others, but what writing and sharing your personal narrative can teach you about yourself' (2004: 124).

## Lifelines

Where to begin? Many authors suggest that before you start to write your educational autobiography, you should construct a 'lifeline', or what is also sometimes called a 'timeline' (see Monteagudo 2005: 6; Sewell and Newman 2006: 5). A lifeline is a well known technique in counselling and provides a pictorial representation of the key events in both your personal life and, in this case, your education, although it could be any other sphere of life.

---

### Activity 1.3
### Describing your lifeline

Draw a horizontal line across a page, dividing the line into years, starting with your birth and taking you forward to five or more years into your future.

Below the line, link dates with significant events in your life such as starting school, moving house, leaving home. The more significant events are placed furthest away from the line (rather as you would do on a graph).

Above the line, map out your educational experience in a similar fashion, again with the more significant events and achievements placed furthest away from the line.

Now reflect on those experiences and the links between them. Consider how your educational experiences have been influenced by external factors and also how your education has influenced your development and progress.

Look into the future and consider where you want to be and what you want to achieve, particularly in terms of your education.

---

## Your educational autobiography

What next? According to Kehily, we all have a number of 'well worn stories we tell about ourselves' and that in writing your autobiography you should begin by:

> . . . tapping into the store of ready-made narratives that individuals select, structure and relate at appropriate moments . . . (while recognizing that) parts of the narrative could be omitted, embellished, reframed and adapted for different audiences. (Kehily 1995: 24)

Thus your lifeline, and the anecdotes and tales that you tell others about your schooldays, become the starting point for mapping out your narrative journey. Another useful staring point is to frame your deliberations about your educational experiences around the answers to a number of questions, starting with rather broad responses and gradually exploring each question in greater depth. Rousmaniere (2000) suggests a number of processes that can provide a useful starting point for more thoughtful remembering, such as:

- describing your favourite teacher
- recalling a good lesson
- considering what part friendships played in your experiences
- describing your school context and how it affected your experience

---

### Activity 1.4

Consider each of these questions and the answers that you give. Try to explain why you can remember some things and not others – what made certain incidents important to you? What do they tell you about yourself?

---

When you start writing 'your self' you have a choice in how you approach constructing your narrative. After all, this is your unique story. Monteagudo (2005) suggests that the narration of an individual's learning journey could be divided into a number of stages that correspond to the phases of formal education. Other suggested approaches include a focus on the different contexts in which learning has taken place or tracing your journey through an exploration of a series of critical incidents or via a montage of pictures. While the structure is obviously important in that it frames the story, what is possibly of more importance is that you reflect critically on your experience and the meanings you attribute to it. In so doing, as Monteagudo suggests, you will eventually arrive at an understanding of yourself:

> . . . at the 'I' and those many different types of 'I': the unusual, the hidden, that perceived by others, the wished for (and) the public . . . (Monteagudo 2005: 8)

---

### Activity 1.5
### Writing your educational autobiography

The following format for writing your educational autobiography is based on one provided by Karpiak (2000: 47).

Think of an apt title for your 'story'.

Divide your story up into about five chapters, providing a separate title for each chapter.

⇨

### Activity 1.5—cont'd

Write two pages for each chapter. Try to avoid writing a simple chronology of events, remember to reflect on your experiences.

Try to link the chapters using a metaphor or some form of thread like the use of (a) picture/s.

Remember to contextualize your experiences, relating them to the wider social and educational context and also to relevant literature.

Finally, using the examples in this chapter as a guide, as you go through the different sections of this book, try to explore your personal experiences from the perspective of some of the key themes we address. For example, consider aims, philosophies and contexts.

# Summary

The telling of ordinary people's life stories with respect to their education is becoming an important aspect of some forms of educational research. It is also becoming an important aspect of some undergraduate programmes, particularly those focused on teacher education. Karpiak suggests that autobiographical writing can be useful because it can enhance learning:

> Because autobiography involves not only recounting memories and expressions but also finding their larger meaning, and to the extent that the activity expands the individual's knowledge of self and the world, it constitutes learning. (1993: 34)

### Key references

Blair, M., Holland, J. and Sheldon, S. (eds) (1995), *Identity and Diversity: Gender and the Experience of Education: A Reader*. Berkshire: OUP.

Mitchell, C. et al. (eds) (2005), *Just Who Do We Think We Are? Methodologies for Autobiography and Self Study in Teaching*. London: Routledge Falmer.

# Part Two
## The Nature of Education

# The Purpose of Education ▪2

## What is education?

At first glance, the answer to this question appears simple – after all, we have all had experience of education in some form or another and are therefore very familiar with the term. When asked the question, 'What is education?' most people generally formulate a response that includes references to the formal process of schooling and the gaining of academic qualifications. Education is also often equated with learning and the acquisition of knowledge, understanding and the skills that will equip an individual for success in their future life. However, as we start to explore the concept of education, we will begin to see that its nature is a highly contentious subject and one that has challenged philosophers and scholars since the time of Plato. Shudak suggests that 'education is certainly a curious thing' (2006: 17) due, on the one hand, to an almost mundane familiarity with the term and on the other, to the academic debate surrounding the meaning of the concept. Hanley (2006) points out that the meaning of education is dependent on both context and perspective, while Harris goes further and suggests that education is 'a changing, contested and often highly personalised, historically and politically constructed concept' (1999: 1).

It is debated as to whether the word 'education' derives from the Latin word *educere* – meaning to 'lead out' or 'bring forth' – or from the word *educare* meaning 'to rear' or 'bring up' (Barrow and Woods 2006: 115). Contemporary dictionary definitions refer to education as the 'bringing up' or 'rearing of a child' together with the notion that this includes mental and moral training. According to Vanderstraeten, 'the idea of education implies that educators (parents, teachers) have the possibility to effect change in those at whom their educational efforts are directed.' However, as he goes on to point out, 'education does not therefore create or produce its own object. Education rather *intervenes* into autonomous processes such as growth and development that are always already occurring' (2006: 160).

R. S. Peters in his text *Ethics and Education*, first published in 1966, suggests that for something to be called education it must be:

- purposeful
- concerned with learning – the transmission of knowledge
- worthwhile
- conducted in a morally acceptable way so that individuals are not coerced, indoctrinated or brainwashed (see Bartlett and Burton 2007: 12; Marshall 2006: 34)

More contemporary writers, such as Gregory, have also attempted to map out the concept of education in a similar fashion. While suggesting that we can agree on how to characterize education, Gregory, too, argues that education is essentially 'a good thing' and that it has a unified and coherent purpose that is directed at developing an individual's capacity to become autonomous. Like Peters, Gregory views education as an essentially cognitive enterprise in which individuals develop the capacity to think rationally and are enabled to make sense of the world in which they live (Gregory 2002 in Davies et al. 2002: 7, 17). Inherent in both perspectives, however, is the notion that education can be characterized as both a product (the something worthwhile) and a process (learning).

The views expressed by both Peters and Gregory about the criteria that define an activity as education have been criticized by other scholars. White (1982), for example, rejects the kind of analyses that Peters, and later, Gregory, attempt in order to develop an understanding of the nature of education, suggesting that a focus on what education is, lacks a consideration of what education is for. As a consequence, White considers that our understanding of what education is for, must inform our view of what education is. He, therefore, suggests an alternative perspective, in which education is viewed simply as 'upbringing':

> In asking what the aims of education ought to be, I shall be taking this to mean: what should we aim at in bringing up children or young people? What kinds of achievements, of character, intellect or whatever, should we wish them to possess? (White 1982: 5)

While the nature of education remains contested, scholars are, however, agreed that education is an intentional and purposeful activity and that the knowledge, skills, attributes and behaviours that pupils gain as a consequence of being educated are valuable both in an intrinsic and in an extrinsic sense.

It is possible that in your reflections on the nature of education you came to the same conclusion reached by many scholars, that is, that in essence education is one of those concepts that appear to defy a single definition. In the following sections, we will attempt to articulate some of the debates that surround the concept of education from a variety of perspectives and develop an understanding of the aims of education for both the individual and the society in which they live.

# What is education for?

## The purposes and aims of education

The purposes and aims of education, like the nature of education, are a contested territory, and Harris suggests that, like the concept of education, they '. . . are social, historical, ephemeral and changing' (1999: 3). As White points out, 'education should be aimed at *something*, even though there are disputes about what that something should be' (1982: 6). Education can be seen to perform an important 'multilayered' *purpose* within society, influencing, or being influenced by, not only an individual's needs and values, but also many other aspects of the society in which they live, such as the economy and politics (Ranson 1994: 4). Individuals differ greatly in the values they hold and in their needs and aspirations, and thus what they perceive to be the purpose of education may vary considerably. Religious background, social status, gender, ethnicity and the stage of education together with a host of other factors can influence what an individual thinks education should be for. The lack of a consensus value system within society also means that any consensus with respect to the aims and purposes of education could be viewed as contentious (Gilroy 1999). Individuals, educational institutions and society, therefore, at any particular time may hold either compatible or incompatible views as to what education is for (Harris 1999; Ranson 1994). As Le Métais suggests:

> National values may be neither national nor discrete. As a result, there may be dissonance between the aims of education expressed by legislation or reforms, and those pursued by students, teachers,

> parents, education administrators, and others. It may be difficult for a single educational structure to reflect a diversity of values and aims, and similar conflicts may arise with respect to internal organisation, curriculum, teaching methods and materials and assessment. (Le Métais 1997: 3)

An analysis of some of the literature (see Chitty 2002: 2; Ranson 1994: 4; Standish 1999: 35; White 1982; Wringe 1988: 20) suggests that there is a general consensus about the nature of the functions that education fulfils within society, namely:

1. to meet the needs of the individual in terms of personal development and the achievement of life and career goals
2. to meet the needs of society by enabling individuals to become active citizens and agents of social change
3. to meet the needs of the economy by investing in human capital and preparing individuals for the world of work
4. to promote what is desirable or worthwhile, such as truth, rational thought and the pursuit of excellence

### Aims

The functions or purposes of education are embodied in the aims of individual educational systems, and not only do they tell us what such institutions perceive education to be for, they determine the character of the institutions and everything else about them, from the nature of the curriculum to the form of assessment (Winch and Gingell 1999: 10).

> Aims are easier to define, and may be expressed as objectives, goals and targets. Educational aims may be intrinsic (e.g. contribute to lifelong education, to develop knowledge, skills and understanding for the individual and society) or instrumental (preparing young people for work and contributing to the national economy). They may focus on developing individual qualities or capacities, or on promoting citizenship or a sense of community or safeguarding a cultural heritage or literacy. (Le Métais 1997: 9–10)

White (1982) offers an alternative classification, placing an emphasis on the development of personal autonomy and well-being; the pursuit of knowledge for its own sake; morality and vocational imperatives, while Winch and Gingell (1999: 13) offer the additional categories of liberal and vocational aims. In general, however, aims reflect the main purposes of education and can be classified according to the four main categories highlighted by Le Métais (1997):

- individual
- social
- instrumental
- intrinsic

The main aims of education, based on those categories, are detailed in Table 2.1 (see also Marples 1999; Winch and Gingell 1999; White 1982; White 2002 and Wringe 1988).

**Table 2.1.** The Aims of Education

| Individual | Intrinsic | Instrumental | Social |
|---|---|---|---|
| • Development of autonomy<br>• Maximization of happiness<br>• Promotion of well-being<br>• Provision for moral and intellectual growth<br>• Preparation for life, work and active citizenship<br>• Provision of a secure cultural heritage | • Pursuit of knowledge, understanding, rational thought and truth<br>• Development of autonomy<br>• Provision and preservation of a secure cultural heritage | • Development of autonomy<br>• Preparation for work or vocation<br>• Promotion of active citizenship<br>• Promotion of economic development<br>• Provision and preservation of a secure cultural heritage | • Promotion of justice, equality and equal opportunity<br>• Preservation of a secure cultural heritage<br>• Promotion of active citizenship<br>• Promotion of economic development |

There is considerable overlap between the categories of aims and, as Wringe suggests, 'It is naturally the case that in pursuing one set of our aims sets we often necessarily promote others as well. However, there are differences of emphasis and may, in fact, often be conflicts' (1988: 20). These tensions and conflicts, however, according to Wringe, may be more academic than real.

A quick glance at the aims and mission statements of a variety of schools, colleges and universities clearly highlights that there is a general commitment to what Barrow termed the 'ideal of autonomy' (1999: 18). There is also a commitment to the notion that education's main aim is to provide individuals with the requisite knowledge, skills and attributes so that they can make sense of their world and lead rich and fulfilling lives. As we shall see in the next section, in England a raft of recent legislation, such as the Children's Act (2004), Every Child Matters (2004) and the Children's Plan (2007), has tasked schools with the responsibility of promoting personal well-being as a major aim. Personal well-being, which encompasses notions of personal autonomy, can be viewed as a key component of an individual being able to lead a flourishing life and is an essential educational requirement of a liberal, democratic society (White 2008). However, at the same time, schools and universities continue to come under pressure from a range of stakeholders (students, parents, employers, governments) to promote the instrumental and social-centred aims of education under the aegis of citizenship, civic participation and employability (see also Barrow 1999).

White (2008) suggests that because the tensions and debates about aims remain, such philosophical explorations continue to be relevant to policy-making. Any shift in favour of vocational and societal imperatives inevitably results in the neglect of more child-centred aims such as personal well-being and happiness. Similarly, a consideration of what is often viewed as a rather elitist imperative, the promotion of the intrinsic aims of education, such as the pursuit of knowledge for its own sake, continues to be overlooked.

### National aims for education

Individual countries tend to differ both in terms of their stated aims for education and in how specific those aims are (Tabberer 1997). The aims of any national education system or institution will tend to reflect a country's heritage, and its socio-political structure will determine how the aims of any system, like education, are agreed and implemented at a policy level (Le Métais 1997). The most commonly articulated aims at a national level (see Inca 2007: 10) are those concerned with:

- individual development and the development of personal qualities, values, morals and ethics
- personal well-being – health, physical activity and leisure
- social development, citizenship, community and democracy
- preparation for work
- promotion of equal opportunities and multiculturalism
- development of knowledge understanding and basic skills like literacy and numeracy, together with scientific and technological skills
- ensuring a cultural heritage and literacy
- providing a foundation for future education and lifelong learning
- encouraging parental involvement in education
- providing for special educational needs

Other national aims include the promotion of excellence and raising standards, the promotion of the national economy, emotional and spiritual development, creativity, and the promotion of environmental and sustainable development. Le Métais (1997) suggests that although national values may not change, social and economic circumstances are subject to considerable change, and, consequently, educational aims may have a limited 'shelf life' and thus, over time, cease to have relevance. Our exploration of the changing aims of primary education in England will clearly illustrate this point.

## Changing times, changing aims:
## The aims of primary education

Le Métais (1997) suggests that it is unusual in England to dwell on such things as values and aims, because England does not have a written Constitution or Bill of Rights. Similarly, until recently, the English education system has had no formal aims laid down; however, implicit within the system has been a view about how society should be developed and how that could be achieved. Winch and Gingell comment that one of the reasons the aims were not laid down was because 'the English system, rigidly hierarchical and exclusionary, as it was, together with a very strong commitment to racial superiority and the dominance of other "lesser people" was understandably reluctant to advertise what it was about' (2004: 9). However, times change and over the last century the aims of primary education, whether implicit within the system, or explicitly formulated, have indeed, as Harris (1999) suggested, been ephemeral and changing. The research briefings for the recent Primary Review, which commenced in 2006, present an excellent overview of the changing aims of primary education over the last century, and what follows owes greatly to that work (see Lauder et al. 2008; Machin and McNally 2008; Shuayb and O'Donnell 2008; White 2008).

## Beginnings

The earliest, and possibly only, statement of the aims of elementary or primary education until 1999 was made by Robert Morant (Permanent Secretary to the Board of Education) in 1904 in his introduction to the 'Elementary Code'. According to White, Morant believed that the aim of the elementary school was:

> To form and strengthen the character and to develop the intelligence of children, to assist both girls and boys, according to their different needs, to fit themselves, practically and intellectually, for the work of life. (in White 2008: 5)

This view persisted, embodying as it did an implicit respect for the individual and for equality of opportunity (Le Métais 1997). In the 1930s, the 'Primary School' proper emerged from the old elementary school, and in his report on its inception in 1931, Hadow, suggested that:

> The general aim and scope of the primary school . . . should not be regarded merely as a preparatory department for the subsequent stage but should be planned around the needs of the child at that particular phase in his physical and mental development. It should arouse in the pupil a keen interest in the things of the mind and in general culture, fix certain habits, and develop a reasonable degree of self-confidence, together with a social or team-spirit. (in White 2008: 7)

Because education was not under state control, although the government was able to make suggestions about the aims and purposes of education, it was left to schools and teachers to determine what was taught and why (White 2008). However, as governments started to see the benefits of education both economically and socially, they started to exert a greater influence. Shuayb and O'Donnell (2008) suggest that since the late 1960s, the aims and purposes of primary education in England (and also in the five other countries they surveyed) have gone through a number of distinct phases as a consequence of changes in political, economic and social imperatives:

| | |
|---|---|
| Phase 1 | Focus on the child |
| Phase 2 | Focus on social and economic concerns |
| Phase 3 | Focus on standards and raising achievement |
| Phase 4 | Focus on economic and social imperatives and also individualized and personalized learning |

## Phase 1: Plowden, 1967 and a child-centred approach

In the late 1960s, the Plowden Report took a distinctly child-centred approach to primary education, suggesting an holistic educational experience focused on an individual child's needs and wants. It is evident, as White (2008) suggests, that the Plowden Report had little to say about the aims of education, believing that the articulation of such aims should continue to be left to individual schools and to teachers. A survey of the educational aims of primary schools of the time highlighted this child-centered approach, and the following aims were found to be the most popular:

- children should be happy, cheerful and well-balanced
- they should enjoy school work and find satisfaction in their achievements
- individuals should be encouraged to develop their own ways
- moral values should be taught as a basis of behaviour
- children should be taught to respect property
- they should be taught courtesy and good manners

(Ashton et al. 1975 in White 2008: 9)

### Phase 2: The 1980s, state control and a National Curriculum

In the 1970s, following the economic recession and the oil crisis coupled with the excesses of the child-centred approach as witnessed at William Tyndale School in Islington and further prompted by James Callaghan's seminal speech at Ruskin College, the focus of education switched from addressing the needs of the individual child to addressing the needs of the economy and society. The government put more money into education and consequently, demanded more state control of what went on in schools. In 1988, the Education Reform Act brought primary education under state control and a National Curriculum was introduced. The aims for primary education were the same as those for secondary education and were to:

- promote the spiritual, moral, cultural, mental and physical development of pupils at the school and of society
- prepare pupils at the school for the opportunities, responsibilities and experiences of adult life

(DES 1989: 2)

### Phase 3: The 1990s, concern for standards and a new National Curriculum

In the 1990s, following on from the focus on the impact of education on an individual's future employability and the impact of education on the economy, concerns started to be raised about standards, particularly with respect to literacy and numeracy. According to White (2008), during this period the government also came under increasing pressure from teachers to articulate the purpose of the National Curriculum. As a result, in 1999, a new National Curriculum was produced together with specific strategies for literacy and numeracy. There was also a more explicit statement of aims, values and purposes for the new curriculum articulated under two main aims:

- to provide opportunities for pupils to learn and achieve
- to promote pupils' spiritual, moral, social and cultural development and prepare all pupils for the opportunities, responsibilities and experiences of life

(DfEE/QCA 1999: 10–12)

The more detailed statements of aims, values and purposes outlined in the document were deemed to provide a framework in which schools could develop their curriculum. However, these aims were not statutory and, as White (2008) suggests, as a consequence, they had little or no impact.

### Phase 4: Aims for the twenty-first century

While the aims, purposes and values of education continue to focus on economic and social goals together with a commitment to raising standards, there has also been an increasing refocusing on child-centred aims with the development of individualized or personalized approaches to learning. This has resulted in what Shuyab and O'Donnell term a 'hybrid of economically driven learner centred and societally engaged aims' (2008: 29). This, they suggest, appears to many as a rather contradictory approach, with, for example, the 'Primary National Strategy' (2003) focusing on excellence and the raising of standards and attainment on the one hand, and on making education enjoyable and meeting the individual child's needs on the other.

In 2003, the government introduced the Every Child Matters: Change for Children initiative. This, together with the Children's Act (2004), heralded a new approach to looking after the well-being of children, arising as it did out of the scandalous case of the neglect and death of little Victoria Climbié. The 'Children's Plan' (2007) further detailed how the changes would be implemented. A total restructuring of all children's services in England is proposed, committed both to excellence and equality and with a view to achieving the following five major aims for children (DfES 2004):

- be healthy
- stay safe
- enjoy and achieve
- make a positive contribution
- achieve economic well-being

Thus, as Shuayb and O'Donnell suggest in their conclusions:

> The aims, values and purposes of primary education today combine the requirements to prepare children for their economic role in society, with the need to identify their individual strengths and weaknesses, so as to provide them with the necessary support to achieve targets. Child-centredness is thus being adapted not only to ensure the individual child's growth, but also to prepare him or her to fulfil their economic role. (Shuayb and O'Donnell 2008: 25)

### The future

In 2007, the government introduced a revised Secondary National Curriculum for Key Stages 3 and 4. The aims of the new curriculum incorporate the five aims of Every Child Matters and, while still recognizing the importance of individual subject studies, place a greater emphasis on life skills and employability. These aims are, for the first time, statutory aims and it will be interesting to see how schools interpret the curriculum in that light. There are also non-statutory programmes of study that relate to the development of personal and economic well-being, drawing together aspects of personal, social and health education (PSHE) with sex education, careers, financial capability, work related experience and enterprise. The three aims of the new curriculum (each of which has a more detailed subset of aims, see DfCSF 2007) are to produce:

- **successful learners** who enjoy learning, make progress and achieve
- **confident individuals** who are able to live safe, healthy and fulfilling lives
- **responsible citizens** who make a positive contribution to society

It is assumed that these aims will become the aims of a new primary curriculum, which is being informed by the research findings and conclusions of the Primary Review. They clearly embody a hybrid of the child-centred, economic and social aims believed to be essential in order for an individual to live and work in a modern, multicultural and fast changing world. However, as White points out, they continue to lack a clear rationale and statement of purpose and thus may remain just an 'ordered list' (2008: 13).

---

### Activity 2.2

Look up the mission statements and statements of aims and purposes of a range of institutions including for example:

- your local primary and high schools
- an independent school
- a Steiner or Montessori school
- a university or further education college

What do the statements tell you about those institutions? For example:

- What do they view the purpose of education to be?
- Are their aims instrumental, intrinsic, social or vocational or do they present a 'hybrid' of aims?
- What kind of education do they provide and how is that reflected, for example in the form of the curriculum and in approaches to teaching and learning?

Finally, reflecting on what you have read, what do you think the aims of education should be? Do you think it is possible for education to be 'aims free'?

---

# Education as a product and a process

The term education is inextricably linked with the process of learning and, in fact, schools are often referred to as 'institutions of learning'. As humans, we have a great capacity to learn. From birth, we are biologically programmed to make sense of the world in which we live and to adapt and respond to changes in our environment. Our large brains, intelligence and capacity for rational thought are considered to set us apart from other members of the animal kingdom, and we are, therefore, often surprised at the ability of our nearest animal relatives, the great apes, to demonstrate such capacities. As human societies have grown, so too has our collective knowledge and understanding and, therefore, in order to preserve and build on our combined cultural experiences and heritage, our learning has become increasingly more formalized, structured and institutionalized.

*So what is learning?* Learning is often considered as a product, that is, the outcome of a process that brings about change in an individual (Smith 1999). *Learning as a product* relates to the gaining of new knowledge, skills, abilities, attitudes or behaviours that influence and change how an individual understands, perceives and responds to the world around them. *Learning as a process* can be defined, therefore, as an essentially cognitive activity because it involves the internal, mental processing of new information in the brain and the formation of memory that results in that change in perception or response. Numerous theories have been proposed to explain how people learn, the differences in individual learning styles, differences in the capacity to learn and in motivation for learning. A huge variety of approaches to teaching and, consequently, learning, have been devised in response to these different learning theories. Learning is no longer considered to be a 'property' of childhood, it is perceived as a continuum, a lifelong process that can take place anywhere and at any time, in sharp contrast to its traditional confinement to formal institutions such as schools.

The UNESCO report on 'Education for the twenty-first century' established a number of important principles for learning throughout life, and defined what they termed the 'four pillars of learning':

- learning to do
- learning to know
- learning to live together
- learning to be

In so doing, they placed the more practical aspects of learning, such as learning how to learn, alongside the moral and ethical aspects of learning, including the development of self-respect and tolerance of others (Greenaway 1999: 3).

*So what is learning* in the context of our understanding of the concept of education? If we go back to our original deliberations, you will recall that both Peters and Gregory perceived education to be an essentially cognitive activity that was purposeful, worthwhile and carried out in a morally acceptable fashion. We have established that learning is a cognitive activity because it influences or changes the way we understand, perceive or respond to the world around us. Therefore, in establishing if what has been learnt is educative, one needs to establish both purpose and value for the activity and be certain that no indoctrination, brainwashing, or coercion was involved. According to Smith (1999: 3), one of the essential questions to consider, therefore, is whether individuals are conscious of what is going on when they are learning. Similarly, one needs to establish that they are willing participants in that learning experience.

## Acquisition learning and formalized learning

In order to distinguish 'educative learning' from 'ordinary everyday learning' it is useful to consider the distinction suggested by Rogers (2003 in Smith 1999) between 'acquisition learning' and 'formalized learning'. Acquisition learning is unconscious or implicit learning, where the learner is not aware that learning is actually taking place. Such learning happens all the time, for example when we learn to carry out simple tasks within the home or we learn to kick a ball. Acquisition learning is really the accumulation of experience. Formalized learning, on the other hand, is 'educative' learning, in that it is guided and purposeful and the learner is conscious that learning is taking place. Rogers (2003 in Smith 1999) suggests that there is a continuum of learning experience, from acquisition learning to formalized learning, all of which can be found in schools.

It is this distinction between activities that are educational and those that are not that forms the basis of the following discussion on the relationship between education and schooling. Davies (2002: 22) suggests, however, that learners rely on far more than cognitive experiences and that there is a danger in restricting all educational activity to cognitive processes because this may result in education being perceived merely as an academic enterprise.

# Education and schooling

The terms education and schooling are often used synonymously. But are education and schooling really the same thing? Schools are certainly places, particularly in developed countries with compulsory mass education systems, where children and young people undertake the majority of their *formal* education. However, it is obvious that schools also perform numerous functions that are, by definition, not educational (Barrow and Woods 2006). Some philosophers of education like Gregory, therefore, suggest that:

> There is a key distinction to be drawn between education and *schooling*, the vehicle through which we seek, in the main, to realise our educational goals and purposes. The activity (or task) of education is laid upon schools. They are judged as being more or less successful at that task. Whatever our ambitions are in educating the young, schools (for reasons bound up with the kind of institutions they are) might not be as successful as we would like. We need to remind ourselves that schools might well serve purposes that owe little to education and its aims. The outcomes of education and schooling are not necessarily coincidental. In short, education and schooling are not the same, even if schools can (and do) go some way to realising our educational ambitions.
> (Gregory 2002: 4)

Barrow and Woods (2006: 12) suggest that as well as educating children, schools fulfil a number of other purposes that could be considered to be simply the 'by-products' of an education system. Although vital components of schooling, they are not considered to be compatible with a liberal view of what constitutes education. For example, some of the activities that take place in school are not considered to be educational because pupils have to learn to do them, or carry them out, simply in order for the school to function efficiently – for example having to learn the school's rules. Others are not consistent with a view of education because, although they may be of value to an individual, they could take place more effectively outside school, for example vocational training. Likewise, there are a number of activities that take place in school that could be of no real value to an individual, and could be considered potentially harmful to their future well-being (Winch and Gingell 1999: 212, together with references). Such activities include child minding; categorizing or stereotyping individuals, for example as clever or hardworking; training individuals in basic skills, for example forming letters and socializing individuals by developing behaviours and cultivating views (Barrow and Woods 2006).

Although a lot of what goes on in schools is not, therefore, by definition strictly education, schools and schooling remain the primary vehicle for the 'education' of the vast majority of people. The contribution to an individual's education and lifelong learning from a variety of other formal and informal contexts, however, cannot be denied, and we will be looking at the contribution that such contexts can make in a later chapter.

## Summary

We started the chapter with two questions: 'What is education?' and 'What is it for?' and it has become obvious, throughout our discussions, that the answers to those questions are not as simple as they first appeared. As we have seen, education, its nature, aims and purposes, are open to a range of interpretations that are, as Harris suggests, rather personal constructs that are dependent upon individual values and context. Conceptual analyses of education, such as those undertaken by Peters and Gregory, have resulted in the defining of the attributes of education rather than education per se. As a consequence, it is generally accepted that for any endeavour to be called 'education', it must be intentional, purposeful and carried out in a morally acceptable fashion. In such analyses, education is conceived as a process, that is learning that results in a product in the form of educational achievements that possess an intrinsic value. Others, like White (1982), are critical of such analyses and take a more pragmatic approach, suggesting that we should focus on what 'education is for' rather than trying to attach a meaning to a concept that is so ephemeral in nature and dependent on individual values and interpretation. White suggests that education equates to 'upbringing' and that we determine its nature and purpose when we determine what kinds of qualities we wish our children and young people to possess.

Education is often seen as a preparation for life or increasingly as education for life (Barrow and Woods 2006). It is considered to be concerned with individual fulfilment and the development of an individual's personality and their potential. However, there is a danger in focusing on such individual outcomes, what Hargreaves termed the 'fallacy of individualism', and in suggesting that:

> If only our schools can successfully educate every individual child in self-confidence, independence and autonomy, then society with confidence can be left to look after itself. (Hargreaves 1982: 93 in Chitty 2002: 2)

## Key references

Barrow, R. and Woods, R. (2006), *An Introduction to the Philosophy of Education* (fourth edition). London: Routledge.

Davies, I., Gregory, I. and McGuinn, N. (2002), *Key Debates in Education*. London: Continuum.

## Useful websites

www.inca.org.uk
  The internet archive of the International Review of Curriculum and Assessment Frameworks
www.primaryreview.org.uk
  The Primary Review – an independent and wide-ranging enquiry into the condition and future of Primary Education in England
www.unesco.org
  United Nations Educational, Scientific and Cultural Organization (UNESCO)

# What It Means To Be Educated  3

## What it means to be educated

Like many concepts in education, that of the 'educated person' is the subject of considerable debate. Our understanding of what it means to be educated changes over time and has both historical and cultural connotations. Levinson et al. (1996: 3) provide us with the notion of a 'culturally variable educated person' and the attributes they are considered to possess are viewed as a product of the prevailing needs of the society and culture in which they live.

In the past, the notion of an educated person has generally been conceptualized from the perspective of the dominant elite and, therefore, linked to specific types of educational experience, social class and the possession of certain attributes. The educated person was considered to be someone, usually male and white, of 'good breeding' who was well read, with a wide range of knowledge, self reliant and who possessed a range of moral virtues that included, according to White, 'prudence, courage, temperance, benevolence, . . . lucidity, independence of mind, wisdom, humour and vitality' (1982: 121).

Peters, in the 1960s, not only sketched out his criteria for the concept of education, but also those of an educated person. Barrow and Woods (2006: 32) provide a critique of Peters' criteria, which suggest that for someone to be considered educated they must:

- be knowledgeable, not just knowing facts but possessing a depth and breadth of understanding of that knowledge within a conceptual framework

- have been transformed by the knowledge they possess, thus informing their outlook on life
- be concerned for the maintenance of the standards of evidence used to justify knowledge in their specific fields

Inherent in this view is the notion that the body of knowledge that the educated person gains is dependent upon the culture in which the individual lives. For Peters, an educated person possessed a liberal education, which included the study of disciplines such as maths, science, arts, literature, history, etc. Peters' concept of the educated person has, however, been criticized. In the 1980s, his views came under attack from feminist critics, who felt that, because in the past women, and also the members of certain ethnic groups and people with disabilities, were often unable to aspire to an education, the conception of the educated person had taken on a peculiarly masculine ideal (Martin 1981).

> In sum, the intellectual disciplines into which a person must be initiated to become an educated person *exclude* women and their works, *construct* the female to the male image or *deny* the truly feminine qualities she does possess. (Martin 1981: 101)

Martin (1981), therefore, suggested that more 'feminine' attributes such as emotional intelligence, interpersonal skills, supportive and nurturing abilities and intuition were lacking from the descriptions. Later critiques, by Barrow and Woods (2006) for example, while accepting Peters' notion that an educated person is in some way transformed by the knowledge and understanding that they gain from their education, suggest that we are still left considering which types of knowledge and understanding are to be promoted.

## Activity 3.1

Many people consider someone to be an educated person not on the basis of the quality of their education or the level of the qualifications they hold, but on the kinds of qualities they possess. What do you consider to be the distinguishing characteristics of an educated person?

- Do you think we should distinguish between different types of knowledge – does a knowledge and understanding, for example, of science count, but not a similar level of knowledge and understanding, say, of cookery?
- Does the level of education, or the kind of educational experience, matter? Is there a 'minimum' level of qualification and can an educated person be self taught?
- Is knowledge and understanding the only defining characteristic? If not, what other attributes and skills do you consider to be important for an educated person to possess?
- Do you think that in defining an educated person we also need to consider the way people look and dress, the way they speak, their behaviour and conduct, their social class, race or gender?
- What about technology? Does our educated person need to have a mastery of contemporary technologies as well?

The next question that we need to address is what kind of characteristics our educated person will need in the future. What kind of attributes will they have to possess in order to cope with a fast changing world, the challenges of globalization and the demands of new technologies? Burbules (2002: 20–23) suggests an alternative vision of the educated person, portraying them as an individual who:

- Has a mastery of learning, rather than a mastery of a particular subject or body of knowledge. This includes the ability to acquire new knowledge and understanding, be receptive to new ideas, be reflective, curious and to think in different ways.
- Is a 'citizen of the world' and possesses a kind of 'educational cosmopolitanism', understanding and appreciating other cultures and alternative world views, together with the ability to see things from another cultural perspective.
- Possesses a strong, but not fundamentalist, commitment to a set of moral values.
- Has the ability to reason.
- Has a 'problem solving disposition' but is also aware of the uncertainty of any outcomes.

Burbules' concept of the educated person raises two interesting questions. First, as he points out, there is the question of what kinds of educational institutions or other educational experiences will be needed to produce our future educated person. Second is the issue of whether our notion of 'cultural variability' should be replaced with a concept of the 'globally educated person'.

# The value of education

The term educated person is an 'evaluative term, generally used commendatorily' (Barrow and Woods 2006: 31) and the underlying criteria that define the educated person can be used to rate or grade people (ibid). There is a general consensus among scholars that education and being educated is a 'good thing' and that the products of education (going back to Peters' conditions), namely the transformation brought about in an individual, the new knowledge and understanding gained as a consequence of the educational experience or the qualifications that are achieved, are both valuable and worthwhile. However, our perspective on whether education can be viewed as a 'good thing' or whether what has been learnt is 'valuable and worthwhile' is, as Davies (2002: 19) points out, dependent on our understanding of what education is for, which in turn is dependent on our view of the relationship between the individual and the society in which they live. Matheson suggests that one of the criteria that could be used to establish that something is educationally worthwhile is *need*, pointing out that:

> What I want is not necessarily what I need and vice versa; this goes for everything I could possibly want or need, and that includes knowledge . . . it is a matter of perspective and relative importance. With this in mind, needs can be defined in terms of societal needs or individual needs.
> (Matheson 2008: 8)

## The value of education to society

Any society would, we assume, *need and want* its individual members to be well educated and highly skilled in order for the society to be economically competetive. As a consequence, a huge emphasis is placed on the importance of education for both the development of individual potential and for developing economic prosperity. The vast sums of money that are ploughed into educational institutions are testament to this fact. The 29 countries that are members of the Organisation for Economic Development and Co-operation (OECD) spend an estimated 6.2 per cent of their collective Gross Domestic Product on educational institutions and are increasingly dependent on the supply of educated people for their economic well-being (OECD 2007).

Societies that invest in education tend to prosper both in terms of increased economic growth and from the greater social cohension that arises as a result of the shared values that are perpetuated through the education system. State-funded education systems, therefore, tend to focus on those aspects of education, the subjects and qualifications, that are most suited to producing a workforce that can provide for economic growth. As a consequence, in England we have seen, first, a shift away from the traditional, classical curriculum with an emphasis on the arts, to one more focused on science, technology and skills. More recently, there has been a drive to introduce more 'creativity' into the curriculum, consequent upon the growth in economic importance of the so-called 'creative industries' (such as music, film and the new digital media). This has occurred in concert with the development of a raft of vocationally orientated qualifications designed to meet the country's future economic needs and to complement the more traditional academic focus of A levels. Similarly, what society views as worthwhile knowledge, is changeable and, as Matheson points out, dependent upon 'whether we seek cultural replication, maintenance or renovation or even replacement' in the kind of society we wish to develop in the future (Matheson 2008: 5).

## The value of education to the individual

The importance of education to the individual, on the other hand, is manifest in the amount of time and effort invested in it and the financial sacrifices made to obtain a 'good' education. However, understanding individual *needs and wants* with respect to education is complex. For many individuals, education is solely aimed at employability and enabling them to get a good job, for example as an accountant or a doctor. The longer the educational experience, the higher the level of qualification, then the greater the job prospects and the rewards – or so the mantra goes. A recent review of research suggested that children conceived their primary schooling mainly in such instrumental terms, viewing the main purpose of education at this stage to be to equip them with the necessary skills in preparation for secondary schooling and eventually for employment (Robinson and Fielding 2008: 7).

Machin and McNally (2008) highlight the fact that about 2 per cent of adults in England are not functionally literate. They suggest that this has serious consequences, not only for the individual's well-being, but for society as a whole, pointing to evidence from the research that highlights the impact of the lack of an education on crime, health and levels of civic engagement. Failing to acquire such basic skills as literacy and numeracy can impact greatly on future employment prospects and wage levels. In the UK, the minimum invest-ment or 'education expectancy' for a basic level of secondary education is 12 years, rising to, on average, 20.7 years for a degree level education. However, the personal benefits from that investment can be great, with higher wages from employment and a consequently improved quality of life. When future earning prospects are compared to the individual cost of education, there is an 8 per cent return from a tertiary level education and an even higher return, particularly for males, for gaining upper secondary level qualifications such as A levels (OECD 2006).

A good education and excellent qualifications are, however, not necessarily essential for an individual's wealth and/or happiness, although the evidence suggests that they do help. The question remains, therefore, are the other possible 'products' of education, such as happiness, physical and mental well-being and socialization – although possibly more or equally valuable and worthwhile to the individual – really viable outcomes of education? If it is possible for schools to promote such things, it is even more dificult to quantify them, and there is a danger that the making of statements about such aims by institutions could be viewed as mere empty rhetoric.

The worth or value of an individual's education to society is inextricably linked to the state's recognition of what an individual has learnt and achieved in the form of qualifica-tions such as A Levels and degrees. Such qualifications not only endorse education as a worthwhile activity in society, but also provide a measure of the value that the state places on the individual's achievement. In general, academic qualifications tend to yield higher wage returns compared to vocational qualifications, particularly low-level vocational quali-fication, and are therefore more valuable in terms of 'employment currency'.

For many individuals, therefore, particularly those who are often referred to as the disaf-fected, education is not a 'worthwhile' experience. It is hard to see how any young person who has spent over 12 years in compulsory education and who leaves unable to read or write prop-erly, without formal qualifications and poor career prospects, can view education as a good thing. In fact, the unemployed often consider that their education was of little help in supply-ing them with the necessary skills needed for employment (Robinson and Fielding 2008).

In some respects, as Davies et al. (2002) point out, the hierarchy of qualifications, in terms of value and worth to society, may be one way in which the state can control access to limited resources, such as highly paid and influential jobs. According to Matheson (2008: 10), this either facilitates social mobility or simply entrenches existing social structures and divides. However, as Rawls points out, when decisions are made about how to allocate educational resources:

> . . . the value of education should not be assessed solely in terms of economic efficiency and social welfare. Equally if not more important is the role of education in enabling a person to enjoy the

culture of his society and to take part in its affairs, and in this way to provide for each individual a secure sense of his own worth. (Rawls in Noddings 2007: 187)

What we have discussed so far deals exclusively with formal education, i.e. education that takes place within state institutions like schools and universities. Education, however, is not limited to such contexts, and just as happiness and well-being as benefits from formal education are difficult to quantify, so too are the benefits of the informal learning opportunities that also take place.

---

### Activity 3.2

It is worth pausing now to consider the following:

- Should societal needs take precedence over individual needs and ambitions with respect to education?
- Who decides what is worthwhile in education?
- Do you consider that learning about science is more worthwhile or valuable than learning about history? Is learning French more valuable than learning Latin?
- What subjects do you think are worthwhile and should be included in the curriculum?
- Do you think that your education has been a good thing and that it has met your needs and wants?

---

# Education as a human right

Acknowledging the value of being educated both to the individual and to the society in which they live has led nations to strive towards an ideal of universal, free elementary education for all. This universal 'right' to an education was laid down by the General Assembly of the United Nations on 10 December 1948, in Article 26 of the Universal Declaration of Human Rights (UN 1948).

Education is a 'second generation' right, which is social in nature and primarily concerned with equality (Jover 2001; Pimentel 2006). As such, according to Pimentel, the right to an education:

> . . . is recognised as the one which empowers individuals to cope with basic needs, such as health and dignity, which enables the full and free development of his or her personality. Also, education is required for the implementation of the collective right to development – which means that any society depends on the education of its members to enjoy satisfactory conditions of life and fully achieve its goals, to assure that they will be able to fulfil personal needs such as housing, health and food. Education is now recognised as the pathway to freedom, and free democratic society depends on its members' abilities to freely choose, think and express themselves and to actively contribute to the political and social processes in pursuit of their interests. (Pimentel 2006: 5)

In practice, however, social rights such as education are, according to Harris (2005), highly susceptible to economic and social pressures and are often constrained by resources. As Harris points out, this means that even in developed countries, the acknowledgement of a right to education, for example providing for a child with special educational needs, does not always result in those rights being met, simply because the resources to meet the child's need are not available. Similarly, a shortage of resources, for example places in nursery schools, can result in competition, and in such circumstances it is usually the better-educated and wealthier individuals who get access to the resources, thus perpetuating inequalities.

The commitment to free, compulsory education for all, at least at elementary level, has been reaffirmed since 1948 in a variety of treaties, including the 'International Convention on Economic, Social and Cultural Rights' (1966) and the 'Convention on the Rights of the Child' (1989) (Jover 2001). Progress to achieving the commitment to universal education, however, has been slow, and in 1990, the World Conference on 'Education for All' established a goal for achieving universal entitlement by the year 2000. This goal, however, was not achieved, and in 2000, the 'UN Millennium Declaration' established two new Millennium Development goals for education, while the 'Dakar Framework for Action' (to which 164 countries have committed) established a set of six new educational goals to be achieved by 2015 (Colclough 2005). Colclough suggests that the six 'Education for All' goals, adopted in Dakar, reflect the substance of the previous declarations of rights. However, they replace commitments with goals that are in effect more ambitious. The goals are to:

1. expand and improve early childhood care and education
2. provide free and compulsory universal primary education by 2015
3. provide equitable access to learning and life-skills programmes
4. achieve a 50 per cent improvement in adult literacy rates
5. eliminate gender disparities in primary and secondary education by 2005 and at all levels by 2015
6. improve all aspects of the quality of education

(UNESCO 2008)

Although education is a universal human right, it is one that is still denied to the 72 million children who do not attend school. The problem does not only reside with elementary education and there are still a staggering 744 million adults who cannot read (UNESCO 2008). Although participation in education is far from universal, it has increased over the 60 years since the Declaration of Human Rights. Worldwide, in 2008 there were 688 million children enrolled in primary education, an increase of 6.4 per cent since 2005. The largest increases in participation in education have been seen in Sub-Saharan Africa, although there is still a long way to go (UNESCO 2008). Jover (2001) suggests that there are a number of obstacles to everyone achieving their right to an education. These obstacles include:

- **Economic difficulties**
  o poverty – poor households or rural households
  o high fees for education

o indirect costs for books, pencils, uniforms, transport, etc.

o high cost of education – insufficient resources dedicated to it

- **Social difficulties**
  o sexism – gender inequality

  o racism

  o cultural and linguistic discrimination

  o class

  o child labour

  o disabilities

  o lack of understanding of the importance of education, an uneducated mother

- **Political difficulties**
  o war and civil conflicts

  o authoritarian governments and political tendencies

  o fear of having free and critical citizens

  o pedagogical difficulties

  o shortages of schools, teachers, materials, technology, etc.

(Jover 2005: 215; UNESCO 2008)

Tomaševski (2005) suggests, however, that the most prevalent obstacles to everyone being able to realize their right to an education are a commercial approach to education, gender discrimination and school drop-out. For example, the World Trade Organisation's General Agreement on Trade in Services (1995) effectively turned education into a 'commodity' or service. Consequently, although human rights law requires states to provide a free and compulsory primary education, international trade laws permit the sale and purchase of education. The resulting expansion of private, fee-paying education has created a two-tier system that:

> . . . creates inequalities rooted in social class, caste and gender – where public education, in very poor condition due to lack of resources, is only used by those who cannot afford to pay for better quality schooling provided by private institutions. (Pimentel 2006: 8)

Gender disparities in enrolment also continue, particularly in developing countries, with more boys than girls being educated. Although the numbers of girls participating in education are on the increase, there is still a general reluctance in many developing countries to provide girls with an education, and their domestic roles – looking after siblings and contributing to the family income – continue to take precedence. Education is a vital step in the empowerment of women, and as Pimentel points out (2006: 8), women who are educated tend to marry later, have fewer children and their children are healthier and better educated.

What is also of concern is that, although levels of enrolment in education are increasing, there is still a large gap between the level of enrolment and the numbers completing their education (UNESCO 2008). Pimental (2006: 9) highlights a variety of causes that contribute to the large number of children who fail to complete their education, including having to work or help their families, pregnancy, not getting along with teachers or other pupils, or simply a lack of interest. Ensuring that children are able to exercise their right to an education, and that they complete it, is vitally important.

There are, of course, scholars who are critical of what has been termed the 'regime of rights', suggesting that a focus on rights can lead to 'excessive individualism' or a 'neglect of responsibilities' (see references in Freeman 2000: 279). In particular, the issue of children having the right to being involved in decisions about their education and other aspects of their well-being, together with notions of children's responsibilities, have been the subject of considerable debate (Freeman 2000; Harris 2005; Wyse 2003). According to Harris (2005), the rights of parents with respect to education have tended to take precedence over the rights of children. It is assumed that parents 'know what is best for their children', while children are often considered incapable of rational thought or unable to articulate their needs and wants. While many parents do take notice of their children's preference when selecting a school, in the main, parents base their choice of school on academic success or on local perceptions of pupil behaviour. Parents also have the right to exclude their children from religious education, religious assemblies and from sex education classes, despite the wishes of their children (Harris 2005).

While 'parent power' has been a prominent feature of education rights, the voice of the child, with respect to their education, is now being listened to. Children are increasingly becoming involved in decision-making, through school councils and youth forums (Harris 2005; Wyse 2003), and, as we shall see in Chapter 5, the rights of the child have been central to the Labour government's reorganization of children's services and the Every Child Matters, Change for Children agenda.

# Summary

Our conception of an educated person is both historically and culturally constructed, their defining attributes emerging out of the needs of the society in which they live. Traditional definitions of what it means to be educated tended to focus on the types of knowledge, understanding and moral virtues that an educated person must possess, while our view of the educated person of the future stresses their ability to learn, to adapt, to reason and to change. What is not contested, however, is the value of being educated for both the individual and to the society in which they live. While being educated can have an intrinsic value for an individual, it is generally the extrinsic goals, particularly in terms of more profitable employment, that are stressed. For the state, the economic and social benefits of investing in an educated workforce are obvious. An acknowledgement that the values that accrue from an education should be available to all people, was entrenched in the United Nations Declaration of Human Rights. Yet, although levels of enrolment in education continue to grow, we are still a long way from achieving the goal of universal, free education.

### Key references

Barrow, R. and Woods, R. (2006), 'The concept of education' in *An Introduction to the Philosophy of Education* (fourth edition). Oxford: Routledge.

Wyse, D. (2003), 'Children's rights' in Crawford, K. (ed.) *Contemporary Issues in Education: An Introduction*. Dereham: Peter Francis Publishers.

### Useful websites

www.un.org/overview/rights/html
 The Universal Declaration of Human Rights (1948)
www.unesco.org
 United Nations Educational, Scientific and Cultural Organisation for details of 'Education for All'

# The Structure of Education 4

# Historical perspectives

Education and schooling are not a modern phenomenon. As civilizations grew and became more complex, it became impossible to record and transmit knowledge simply through traditional oral means. More formal and structured forms of instruction and education became necessary, aided first by the development of writing, and later by the development of books. The ancient Greeks, although not the first society to provide education, adopted a humanistic view in which education was a means of preparing their children for their future role as citizens. By around 400 BC, the first schools had been established in Greece and, aided by great thinkers such as Socrates, Plato and Aristotle, and mathematicians like Euclid, the study of subjects such as philosophy and geometry developed. The Romans continued the Greek tradition but shifted the emphasis in the curriculum towards language and speech-making.

By the middle ages, the notion of educating all citizens had disappeared, but the remnants of those early education systems could be found in churches and monasteries, where children were educated in Latin to become priests or clerks. Education was also provided by charity schools and orphanages. For the rich, there was privately funded education. Young noblemen were taught the art of chivalry, while others learnt a trade as an apprentice to a craftsman. The middle ages also witnessed the emergence of the universities like Oxford and later,

Cambridge. The sixteenth century, the renaissance period, saw a return to the humanist tradition established by the Greeks. However, education remained mainly an elite pursuit.

During the seventeenth and eighteenth centuries, education continued to be provided by the church, in parishes and monasteries, and remained generally inaccessible to the poor. During this period, however, educational pioneers like Rousseau (see Chapter 7) started to influence educational thinking. The forces of rising industrialization and increasing urbanization demanded a better educated population. Education began to be seen as a vehicle for social reform, and there were demands to increase educational opportunity and provide universal schooling (Pimentel 2006).

## Modern education systems

The roots of modern education systems can, therefore, be found in the developing provision for education in mid-nineteenth century Europe and America, particularly in Germany. As compulsory state schooling grew, it replaced, or was integrated into, existing educational provision (Soysal and Strang 1989: 277). We have now largely rejected the traditional, functionalist perspective that the expansion of mass schooling arose as a mechanism for socialization and social control in order to maintain the dominance of an economic and political elite, necessitated by the growing complexity of society as a result of the industrial revolution. The development of mass education is now often viewed as a vehicle for developing the newly emerging nation states of that period (Meyer et al. 1992; Soysal and Strang 1989). The following features identified by Benavot et al. (1991 in Meyer et al. 1992: 131) were typical of the emerging Western, mass educational systems:

- socialization of individuals as members of society
- a secular outlook
- universal provision
- an increasingly standardized curriculum
- a linkage of mastery of the curriculum with personal development and with national progress

Mass schooling has now, according to Meyer et al. (1992), become a worldwide phenomenon. The guarantee, or partial guarantee, of a free elementary education is now written into the constitution of 142 countries, although there is still no such right in over 20 per cent of the world's nations (Tomaševski 2001). Enrolment in education is still increasing, with over 86 per cent of the world's children now enrolled in primary schooling, although the ideal of universal, free, primary education is yet to be achieved (UNESCO 2008). The provision of mass primary education has brought about a corresponding increase in enrolment in secondary education. The rise of mass education in the twentieth century has led to the development of largely institutionalized state education systems (Soysal and Strang 1989). Thus:

> . . . although a multitude of different types of schools and educational establishments, supported by a multitude of individuals and corporate actors, had been in existence for centuries – it

was essentially the achievement of universal mass schooling that marked a decisive transition toward the constitution of institutionalized education as a modern 'system'. (Schriewer et al. 2000: 5)

# Orientation and organization

An education *system* refers to the way in which education is organized between the state, society and individuals (Coelen 2003). The structure of any country's education system owes a lot, therefore, to history, socioeconomic circumstances and dominant political ideologies. According to Avenarius and Liket (2000: 26) there are two main ways in which education systems can be organized:

- **State-orientated systems** in which there is:
  o equality of opportunity
  o similar provision for all
  o uniform teacher training
  o a detailed national curriculum
  o strong central regulation
  o teachers as civil servants, transmitting the norms, values and practices of society
- **School-orientated systems** in which:
  o there is acceptance that there are different ways in which educational aims can be met
  o education can be based on individual philosophies or orientated around religious beliefs
  o the curriculum is not prescriptive
  o teachers are not civil servants and can exercise choice over what is taught
  o the quality of the system is ensured through evaluation, in which teachers are involved

Over time, however, systems do evolve and educational systems can, therefore, exhibit a mixture of the two approaches. All education systems also exhibit a number of organizational features, from an overall framework of provision – the 'meta-organization', usually funded by the state – to the 'micro-organization' of individual classroom activities (Schriewer et al. 2000). Such features can be used when comparing systems, however, there is no consensus approach to comparison and analysis (Rix and Twining 2007), but based on a hybrid of typical comparative approaches (Schriewer et al. 2000; see also Riggall and Sharp 2008; Rix and Twining 2007), the following components of an education system emerge:

- **The meta-organization**
  o overall administrative framework
  o the provider, e.g. state, public
  o source of funding
  o the main values, aims and purposes
  o processes

- **The macro-organization**
  - the differing contexts – the types of institutions/schools
  - institutional level vision, purpose and aims
  - the different levels or key stages
  - the nature and structure of the curriculum
  - the assessment framework
  - the organization of the school year
- **The micro-organization**
  - the organization of teaching and learning in the classroom
  - the non-educational functions such as discipline and socialization

Within these levels of organization there are also numerous 'players or actors' who fulfil various roles, and may also be responsible for aspects of provision, within the system. They include the learners, their families, headteachers and teachers, other professionals, government agencies, local authorities, governors, members of the local community, churches and faith groups, voluntary organizations and businesses.

# An open systems perspective

While breaking down educational systems into constituent components in this fashion may be useful for analysis or comparison, a consideration of how the differing components interrelate is possibly of more value. Education systems are very complex, social organizations, with a vast array of functions and processes and numerous internal and external interactions (Chrispeels 1992: 2). Borrowing from ecological theory used to describe the relation between an organism and its environment, an *open systems* model or perspective (Ballantine and Spade 2008; Chrispeels 1992) provides a way of conceiving education systems as a dynamic whole, and also serves to capture some of the complex relationships that exist between the various components. The model is equally valid at both a systems and an institutional level. Figure 4.1 highlights how any education system or single educational institution can be viewed from an open systems perspective.

## Systems and environments

The stated purpose, vision and aims of an education system or institution are central to the model. The system is bound by this ethos, which determines the structure of the system, the institutional contexts, the modes of participation and the roles performed by individuals. The ethos of the system also determines the nature of the curriculum, the framework of assessments and the nature of processes that take place within it, such as the form of the teaching and learning experience and of socialization (Chrispeels 1992).

Although the system or institution has a 'boundary' and can, therefore, be differentiated from other similar systems, in line with our ecological analogy this boundary is perceived

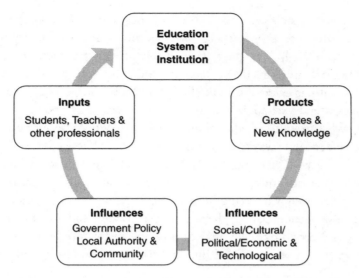

**Figure 4.1.** Education as an Open System (Adapted from Ballantine and Spade 2008: xiv)

as permeable, so that interactions and exchanges with 'the environment' in which the system exists, can occur. There is a huge range of 'environmental influences' on education systems, from those at a local environmental level to more national or even international prerogatives. As Ballantine and Spade point out, educational institutions 'exist within a maze of social, political and legal expectations' (2008: xv). Environmental interactions can, therefore, range from having to respond, on one level, to current government legislation and initiatives such as Every Child Matters, or to advances in technology by increasing the use of 'e-learning', to, on another level, more local issues relating to, for example, parental or community imperatives. The crucial factor, however, is that the 'environment' is different for every institution and, so too, therefore, are their responses. The environment is also constantly changing (Ballantine and Spade 2008: xv) and, as a consequence, to continue with our theme, education systems, like ecological systems can, therefore, be seen to change or to 'evolve' over time.

## Inputs and outputs

As in any ecological system, the interactions with the 'environment' are mediated through the 'inputs' and 'outputs' of the system. All systems and organizations need resources in order to produce their 'products', and education is no different. Some inputs like funding, a supply of students and well-qualified and trained staff, are essential for the 'health' and 'survival' of the system. Other essentials include well-equipped buildings, appropriate teaching materials and efficient support staff.

Because students and staff are drawn from the local community, they too bring with them external environmental influences that determine how the institution functions (Ballantine and Spade 2008). The huge effect of the local environment on an educational institution, particularly in terms of the demographic of the student intake, with regard to social class and wealth, is evidenced in the fact that families will often move house so that their children can attend a school in a locality that is perceived as 'good'.

As students pass through the educational system, they become *outputs*, or products; graduates who have in some way been 'transformed' by the knowledge, skills and qualifications they have gained (Chrispeels 1992). The outputs are dependent, in some respect, on the purpose of the institution, so for example a university will produce not only graduates, but also new knowledge resulting from academic research. As graduates emerge from the system, they too become part of the wider environment and are able to influence its culture, politics and economy. They may also be the instigators of new technologies or ways of thinking. In this way they continue to influence, and also be influenced by, the system.

## Feedback

An important feature of all ecological systems is the existence of 'feedback mechanisms'. In education, the government, headteachers, university vice chancellors, heads of Children's Services and others are constantly responding to the findings of academic research reports, inspection results and the outcomes of assessment regimes. The feedback they receive from such information is used to meet the demands of the system and to inform change in the form of new legislation, initiatives or practice. This ability for *self-reflection* is considered to be a particular characteristic of modern education systems (Schriewer et al. 2000).

The development of an 'audit culture' within education has, however, forced schools to place a greater emphasis on measurable outcomes, such as student performances in standardized tests and also on 'risk management', focusing on child protection, child safety and general health and safety issues. Perry and McWilliam (2007) suggest that this has had a potentially detrimental effect, with schools concentrating on preparing pupils for tests rather than on pursuing other educational goals. This has resulted in what they term 'a reductionist view' of education, in which success is equated with measurable outcomes determined by governments. As a consequence they feel that:

> Schools have become, in many cases, closed systems where externally determined targets drive activity, while the diversity and breadth within and between schools made possible by an open system built around reflective practice have all but disappeared. (Perry and McWilliam 2007: 37)

## The 'ghost of competition past'

Education systems, like environmental systems, are often more a reflection of past 'competitions' between differing environmental influences than a reflection of the 'current state of play'. The 'ghost of competitions past', to coin another ecological phrase (see Connell 1980), that is, the influence of past competing ideologies, political, social and economic imperatives, can often be seen to haunt the system. In England, for example, historical traditions and structures such as Victorian school buildings and the legacies of the 1988 Education Reform Act, together with public nostalgia for the so called 'halcyon days' of public schools and grammar schools, the 11 plus exam and the gold standard of A levels, continue to 'haunt' the system and may make its future proofing very difficult. In Chapter 5, we will examine the English education system in more detail and, as we do so, the 'competition' between the existing system and the measures being taken to bring about change is clearly evident.

# A comparative perspective

The comparative study of education systems owes its origins to the early 'travellers' tales' that provided descriptions of what schools were like in other countries. These early descriptive accounts promoted an interest in the field and led to the development of more systematic descriptions of systems and more scientific methods of analysis (Phillips 2006). The study of education systems worldwide is now termed *Comparative and International Education*. According to Crossley and Watson (2003), it represents the joining of two parallel and complementary approaches to comparing national education systems:

**Comparative education**: The analytical study of educational systems mainly in industrialized countries in the West. Based on an analysis of data collected, comparisons are made of the effectiveness of a variety of educational practices, and the findings can be used to inform the translation of successful policies from one context to another.

**International education**: The applied study of educational systems mainly in developing countries. Education systems are studied within their social, political and cultural context.

## Purpose

Comparative studies of education systems are useful, particularly for governments wishing to evaluate policy options and, therefore, can be seen to fulfil a number of purposes (see Crossley and Watson 2003: 19) that align well with what Arnove (2007: 3; see also Bartlett and Burton 2007) terms the three dimensions of Comparative education:

**The pragmatic dimension:** This is about developing a better understanding of one's own education system and providing suggestions about how to improve or reform current policies and practice.

**The scientific dimension**: This is about developing theories based on identifying similarities and differences between systems, for example in terms of policies and ways of doing things, and also of developing an understanding of the relationship between education and its social, political and cultural context.

**The global dimension:** This is concerned with fostering greater cross-cultural understanding and cooperation.

*Policy borrowing*

On a pragmatic level, as Arnove (2007) points out, one of the main purposes of Comparative education is the borrowing or transfer of policies and their subsequent adaptation from one education system to another. While there are a numerous examples of successful policy borrowing there are also examples of policies that have been hastily and uncritically adopted (see Corner and Grant 2008: 80–181 and Bartlett and Burton 2007: 8–9). In England, examples of policy borrowing include Every Child Matters, which is considered to have been based on 'No Child Left Behind' in the USA, and the notion of 'extended schools', which is based on the 'full service provision' model, again from the USA (see Chapter 10).

## Approaches

Comparative education uses a number of methodologies, depending on the type of study being undertaken. The majority of contemporary studies are either national *case studies* or cross-cultural *thematic studies* that focus on particular aspects of provision, for example the curriculum, school leadership and adult educational provision, to name but a few. Such studies also include the development of models and typologies (Corner and Grant 2008). However, all comparative studies start with the collection of both qualitative and quantitative data, which form the basis of the description of the systems being compared (Oni 2005).

Arnove (2007) suggests that the field of Comparative and International Education has undergone a number of changes in approach and also a number of paradigm shifts, from those early descriptive comparisons, through structural functionialist and world view accounts to post-modernist, post colonial and feminist perspectives. He suggests that there has also been a shift in focus, from a consideration of education systems at the macro-organizational level, considering the whole system and its contribution to, for example, social mobility and economic growth, to a consideration of the micro-organizational level, focusing on what is taught in classrooms and what learners learn. Arnove (2008: 14) suggests that the future directions for Comparative and International Education research include the incorporation of theories of:

- multiculturalism
- social movements
- critical modernism
- critical race theory

## Problems

While there are obvious benefits that can accrue from the study of other education systems, there are a number of problems with adopting an uncritical approach, which include:

**Ethnocentricity and cultural superiority:** People often hold preconceptions about what constitutes a good education system, and their own particular world view and assumptions about the cultural superiority of their own system can often prevent them from viewing other education systems in a completely neutral and objective fashion.

**Misunderstandings:** Confusion can often arise in comparative studies due to the misunderstandings of terms and concepts as a consequence of language barriers and incorrect translations. Also, when comparing national systems it is important to ensure that the same units of comparison are adopted, because many apparent single systems are actually composites of individual countries or states.

**Political justification:** Politicians often use international comparisons to justify educational reform. There is an obvious danger in promoting, for political purposes, the successful implementation of a policy initiative in one country as a rationale for change and then assuming that it will simply transfer from one context to another.

While there are obvious problems with the use of comparative data, comparative studies are becoming increasingly important in the context of globalization:

> . . . the workings of the global economy and the increasing interconnectedness of societies pose common problems for educational systems around the world . . . Although there are common problems – and what would appear to be increasingly similar education agendas . . . (Arnove 2008: 1)

---

### Activity 4.1

There are a number of very useful internet databases that provide current information about all aspects of education provision in a large number of countries. Visit either the 'Eurydice' or the 'Inca' websites and use the information they provide to compare a number of education systems. In particular you could focus on a comparison of the education system in England, which we detail in Chapter 5, with that in other countries. The other countries in the United Kingdom are an obvious choice, while Finland is also worth considering for comparison because of its recent high performance in the PISA study, carried out by the OECD. In your comparisons you may wish to consider:

- the age at which children start school and the length of compulsory education
- the level of state involvement in education provision
- similarities and differences between aims and purposes, phases and key stages, the curriculum, assessment frameworks and post-compulsory education

---

# Summary

In this chapter we have seen that mass compulsory state education arose as a consequence of the building of nation states during the latter half of the nineteenth century. Mass schooling provided such states with a mechanism for socialization and with the ability to link personal development and national progress. As mass state schooling has developed, it has become largely institutionalized in systems that demonstrate differing degrees of state involvement.

Such systems can be studied from a variety of perspectives – from the macro, whole system level to the micro, concerned with what takes place at the classroom level.

Two differing perspectives on educational systems were also considered. An Open Systems Model enables education systems to be viewed in their entirety. Taking the analogy of an environmental feedback mechanism, an educational system is considered as a complex social organization and the method allows the capture of the relationships that exist and the interactions that occur between the various components of the system and its environment. The Comparative perspective on the other hand, allows for the comparison of different national education systems. What emerges from such an analysis is that, while there are overall similarities in the construction and functioning of education systems, there are also local, regional and national differences in the solution to similar problems. In the context of globalization, the study and comparison of education systems becomes increasingly important.

## Key references

Arnove, R. F. and Torres, C. A. (eds) (2008), *Comparative Education: The Dialectic of the Global and the Local* (third edition). Lanham: Rowman & Littlefield.
Ballantine, J. H. and Spade, J. Z. (eds) (2008), *Schools and Society: A Sociological Approach to Education* (third edition). Los Angeles: Pine Forge Press.

## Useful websites

www.eurydice.org/portal/page/portal/Eurydice
    Eurydice is an information network on education in Europe
www.inca.org.uk
    Inca is the internet archive of the international review of curriculum and assessment frameworks
www.oecd.org
    OECD – the Organisation for Economic Co-Operation and Development website
www.tims.bc.edu
    The *TIMSS & PIRLS* International Study Centre at Boston College dedicated to conducting comparative studies in education (see also www.nces.ed.gov)

# The English Education System 5

## Influences

A state education system first emerged in England in the late 1870s. Initially the system developed as a means of filling the gaps where there was no church or charitable provision. There was a great reluctance among politicians for the state to be fully involved in education, a reluctance that continues to this day (Martin 2008). Thus a rather ad hoc mix of publicly funded and privately funded, church and charitable schooling formed the basis of our current education system and its influence still prevails. Since then, political, social and economic imperatives have played a huge part in influencing the structure of the system. In particular, since the 1988 Education Reform Act there has been a huge increase in government legislation, policy initiatives and interventions, all of which have contributed to the system that is in place today. According to Brisard and Menter (2008: 246), within the raft of policies and legislation since 1988, there have been two main contradictory forces at play that have greatly influenced the structure of education in England. So, for example, on the one hand there has been:

- rationalization in terms of:
  - the phases of education
  - 'comprehensivization' – equality of provision

While on the other there has been:

- diversification in terms of provision based on:
  - specialism
  - collaboration

During the same period, education has come under increasing pressure to be more responsive to perceived economic need and social changes, so that issues such as social inclusion, skills shortages, keeping pace with scientific and technological developments, engagement in politics and society and the lifelong learning agenda have also influenced the way in which the system has developed. There has also been a general trend towards developing a more 'consumerist approach' in terms of student choice and a more 'personalized approach' to learning (Le Métais 2002). For some, however, as Jones et al. (2008) point out, there have been rather too many policy initiatives and insufficient time provided for their effectiveness to be accurately assessed:

> . . . primary education . . . has been as bedevilled by a combination of 'moral panics' and 'policy hysteria' as elsewhere in education and beyond. There have been too many initiatives, too much short term response to media engendered scares, involving ever shortening cycles of reform, multiple innovations, frequent policy shifts, an increasing tendency for reforms to become symbolic in nature, a scapegoating of systems, professional and client groups, shifting meanings within the central vocabulary of reforms, an erosion of professional discretion, and untested and untestable success claims. (Jones et al. 2008: 1)

# Meta-organization: Organization and control

## Provision and funding

A free and compulsory full-time system of education is provided in England by the state for all children aged 5–16. Many children, however, enter the education system at age 3–4 when they attend pre-school play groups or reception classes and are entitled to free, state funded, part-time education. Alternative forms of provision (approved by the state) such as a fee-paying, independent school are also available, as is the possibility of being home-schooled (Eurydice 2007/8; Inca 2008). Children in England tend to enter education at an earlier age than in other countries, based partly on historical circumstance and partly on the premise that a longer period of primary education will impact positively on future attainment; however, the latter is not supported by evidence from research (Riggall and Sharp 2008).

## Organizational framework

The English system is typical of a *decentralized system*, and responsibility for educational provision is shared among a number of different agencies (O'Donnell et al. 2007). Currently

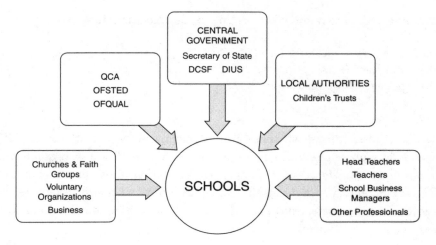

**Figure 5.1.** Influences on Schools.

control lies within a hierarchy of central government and local authority agencies, churches and voluntary organizations, governing bodies and headteachers, all informing the nature and structure of the provision and ensuring its quality and standards within schools as indicated in Figure 5.1.

## The role of central government

Ultimately, the responsibility for educational provision in England lies with the government under the aegis of the Secretary of State for Children, Schools and Families and the Secretary of State for Innovation, Universities and Skills. The development of legislation and guidance is divided between their two departments:

- The Department for Children, Schools and Families (DCSF) is responsible for all aspects of compulsory and pre- and post-compulsory education for children aged from birth to 19.
- Department for Innovation, Universities and Skills (DIUS) is responsible for further and higher education.

## Purpose

The DCSF is committed to 'enabling all children and young people to reach their full potential' and its stated purpose is to 'make England the best place in the world for children and young people to grow up' and to:

- make children and young people happy and healthy
- keep them safe and sound
- give them a top class education
- help them stay on track

(DCSF 2008)

In order to achieve its purpose, the DCSF is, therefore, responsible for the development and implementation of legislation and a variety of initiatives relating to children, schools and families in England. Recent initiatives relating to education have included:

- The Children's Plan (2007)
- The Draft Apprenticeships Bill (2008)
- Shakespeare for all Ages and Stages (2008)

## Aims

As we saw in Chapter 2, the newly stated aims of the English system, at least for pupils during the secondary phase of education, are to ensure that pupils are *successful learners* and become *confident individuals* and *responsible citizens*. These aims operate in concert with the five *ECM* outcomes, which means that the education system is also tasked with ensuring that children are happy, safe, enjoy and achieve, make a positive contribution and are able to achieve economic well-being.

## Curriculum and assessment

The responsibility for ensuring that schools meet those aims and outcomes partly belongs to the Qualifications and Curriculum Authority (QCA), a non-departmental government body that acts as a self-styled 'public champion of the learner' (QCA 2008). The QCA is responsible for the development and review of the national curriculum, its programmes of study, attainment targets and assessment.

## Quality and standards

In line with the government's agenda to move away from more centralized control, new systems have been put in place to ensure the quality of educational provision. There is now a so-called 'New' Ofsted, which is responsible for ensuring that:

- the aims of education are achieved
- standards are maintained in a wide range of contexts, from state schools to childminding settings

For schools, Ofsted now operates a new 'lighter touch' three year inspection cycle and a more self regulatory approach in which schools assess their own performance in terms of:

- the standard and quality of educational provision
- the effectiveness of leadership and management within the school
- how well learners achieve with respect to the five ECM outcomes

The recent controversies surrounding grade inflation at A level and the marking of SATS papers serve to highlight the difficulty of the task of regulating examination boards and ensuring that assessments are fair and valid and that standards are maintained. This role, formerly part of the responsibility of the QCA, is now the jurisdiction of a separate, new independent statutory authority, the Office of the Qualifications and Examinations Regulator (Ofqual), which reports directly to Parliament.

## *The role of local government*

Although government departments are responsible for producing the strategic framework within which schools and other educational institutions operate, and for ensuring the quality and standard of the provision, there has been a gradual shift away from centralized control of the system. The Children's Act (2004) provided the legal underpinning for the complete transformation and reorganization of local authorities' current provision for children's services, including getting rid of the old LEAs, whose sole purpose was education, in order to provide a more integrated and holistic approach to looking after the well-being of children and young people. The details of how the transformation would take place were outlined in the Children's Plan (DCSF 2007). Local authorities have, therefore, established either Children's Services Authorities (CSAs) or what are termed 'Children's Trusts', which bring together, under one umbrella, all the services for children, including education, social services, health and the police.

Children's Trusts are central to government policy for improving children's services and have to produce a local Children and Young People's Plan (CYPP), which highlights their strategic approach to ensuring that the Every Child Matters outcomes for children and young people are achieved. A recent review of a number of CYPPs suggested that, while it was obvious that they were still evolving, there was evidence of considerable diversity in the development of local agency partnerships in response to local needs. There was also a variable usage of the ECM outcomes framework to inform the strategies (Lord et al. 2006).

Children's Trusts, however, are not only tasked with policy development, they also play a role in monitoring performance and improving standards. At a local level, CSAs and Children's Trusts continue to carry out the responsibility for education that used to lie with LEAs, including:

- staffing and staff development
- school meals and transport to schools
- school admissions
- monitoring and improving educational standards
- supporting inclusion and special educational needs
- looking after children in care

(DCSF 2008)

## *A new relationship with schools*

Since 2005, the government has developed a self-styled 'new relationship with schools' that has included:

- less central control
- lighter touch inspections based on self evaluation
- a 'single conversation' with a School Improvement Partner or 'SIP' to produce a 'single development plan' for a school

- delegated budgets
- rationalization of websites and provision of self-service documentation online

(DfES and Ofsted 2004)

The Children's Plan (2007) also presents a new role for schools as the centre of their communities, and demands that more effective links between schools, the NHS and other children's services are made so that, together, they can engage parents and tackle the barriers to the learning, health and happiness of every child. As the Secretary of State who introduced the initiative, Ed Balls, suggests:

> . . . schools need to be able to rely on a strong, supportive network of other services such as housing, health, youth services and the local police if they are to succeed in their core mission. While many schools have strong relationships with their local health services, social services, police, youth centres and sports facilities, many schools still find it more difficult than they should to get support and specialist help when they need it. To do this, schools must have an effective voice in local decisions about how these services work, and getting timely and high-quality support when they need it. It means schools sitting at the heart of public services for children. (Balls 2008)

## *Others*

The Church, faith groups, voluntary organizations, volunteer members of the community in the form of school governors, headteachers and teachers together with the other professionals such as School Business Managers and Learning Mentors who now work in schools, also make a significant contribution to the education system. While churches, in particular the Church of England, faith groups and other voluntary organizations have had a long tradition of involvement in the state education system, business, too, is increasingly playing a part.

---

### Activity 5.1

- Who do you think really controls education?
- Do you think that the notion of totally integrated children's services is really workable? Consider some of the costs and benefits of such an approach.

---

# Macro-organization: Contexts and curriculum

## Contexts and phases

The English education system is divided into four phases that are based on the ages of the children, the type of school provision and the nature of the curriculum:

| | | |
|---|---|---|
| Phase 1 | 0–5 | Pre-school – Early Years Foundation Stage |
| Phase 2 | 5–11 | Primary (compulsory) |

| Phase 3 | 11–16 | Lower secondary (compulsory) |
| Phase 4 | 16–19 | Upper secondary/sixth form/FE or tertiary College |

In some local authority areas a two tier primary/secondary system operates, while in others there is a three tier system: first/middle/secondary; with pupils attending Middle Schools from the ages of 8–12 or 9–13 (Eurydice 2007/8; Inca 2007).

There is a debate concerning the relationship between the various phases and the impact that such relationships have on how each phase is conceived and on what is taught. For example, the relationship between pre-school education and primary education has raised issues of the early age at which children enter primary education in England, and concerns over an increasing focus, particularly in terms of the curriculum and outcomes, on the needs of very young children and in early years provision. In other countries, like Germany, the delayed start to primary schooling means that the curriculum is more skewed towards preparing children for the secondary phase rather than towards early years, as it is in England (see Riggall and Sharp 2008: 14).

Similarly, there is debate about the relationship of the secondary phase to both primary and post-compulsory education. The secondary phase can either be viewed as a 'crossroad in education', that is either a continuation of the primary phase or a preparation for post-compulsory education; or it can be viewed more as a 'link', a part of a continuum, linking primary education with higher education, vocational education and work (Hughes 1998: 4 in Greenaway 1999: 4). While it is acknowledged that the transition from the primary phase to the secondary phase can be very difficult, if the secondary phase is too closely aligned to primary education, this often results in children being ill-prepared for later study, while a closer alignment of secondary education and post-compulsory requirements presents the dual problems of progression and continuity of experience (Greenaway 1999). Further details of the phases as they relate to the different age groups and National Curriculum Key Stages are provided in Table 5.1.

## Phase 1: Early Years Foundation Stage

There is a huge diversity of provision for pre-school children, including private nannies and childminders, private day nurseries, private and maintained pre-school playgroups, Sure Start Children's Centres and Reception Classes in primary schools. Government statistics for 2005/6 demonstrate that around 64 per cent of 3–4 year olds were enrolled in pre-school education within English schools, triple the number in the early 1970s. The rise in the numbers of children in pre-school education within schools, despite the decline in the numbers of 3–5 year olds within the population, is partly due to an increase in early years provision in reception classes fuelled by a combination of insufficient nursery places to meet demand, more favourable staffing ratios in schools and the financial benefits for schools of having more pupils on the roll (Riggall and Sharp 2008). A further 35 per cent of children aged 3–4 were also enrolled in a variety of non-school settings, such as play groups, but these numbers included some children who were also enrolled in pre-school education in schools (National Statistics Online 2007).

**Table 5.1.** Phases and Stages

| Phase | Stage | Year | Age | Type of Institution |
|---|---|---|---|---|
| Pre-School & Nursery Education | Early Years | | 0–4 | Pre-School Settings & Nurseries |
| | Foundation Stage | R | 4–5 | Reception Class in Primary School |
| Primary Education | Key Stage 1 | Y1 | 5–6 | Primary Schools |
| | | Y2 | 6–7 | |
| | Key Stage 2 | Y3 | 7–8 | In some schools: |
| | | Y4 | 8–9 | Key Stage 1 = Infants |
| | | Y5 | 9–10 | Key Stage 2 = Juniors |
| | | Y6 | 10–11 | |
| Lower Secondary | Key Stage 3 | Y7 | 11–12 | Secondary Schools |
| | | Y8 | 12–13 | In some areas: |
| | | Y9 | 13–14 | Middle School for ages |
| Secondary Education | Key Stage 4 | Y10 | 14–15 | 8–12 or 9–13 |
| | | Y11 | 15–16 | |
| | | | 16–18 | Secondary School/ 6th Form College/ Tertiary or FE College |
| Higher & Further Education | | | 18+ | HE and FE Institutions |

*Source:* Based on information available at http://www.direct.gov.uk and http://inca.org.uk

## Phase 2: Primary

Over the past 40 years, the number of children in primary schools in England has varied around the 4 million mark, while over the same period the number of state-maintained primary schools has actually declined from [20,789 in 1965 to 17,762] in 2004 (Riggall and Sharp 2008). The loss, mainly of small and middle schools, coupled with the joining of infant and junior schools, has led to primary schools becoming larger, with on average 224 pupils per school (Eurydice 2006). There are *three categories* of state primary schools (and secondary schools) in England (see Riggall and Sharp 2008):

- community or maintained schools
- voluntary schools – originally funded by the Church or other organizations and now funded by the local authority
- foundation schools – funded by the local authority but owned by the school governors or charities

There is also a *variety of types* of primary school, determined by the age range of the pupils from infant (4–7), first (4–8/9), junior (7–11), primary (5–11) and middle (8/9–12/13). Some primary schools also have play groups or nurseries attached to them (Riggall and Sharp 2008). Children can also attend fee-paying independent schools, many of which follow the practices of particular educational innovators such as Steiner and Montessori. The majority of primary schools are co-educational and children are taught, in general, in mixed ability groups. Since 2002, all schools have been able to form 'federations' with other schools, in order to share leadership and governance. Although the practice is mainly confined to the secondary sector, there are a number of examples of primary schools forming successful federations, particularly with local secondary schools (Riggall and Sharp 2008).

### Phase 3: Lower secondary

During the twentieth century, secondary education, in England as in other developed countries, has gone from a purely academic pursuit for the privileged to a universal and diversified provision (Greenaway 1999). In that time, again in line with other countries (see Benavot 2006: 10), there has also been:

- a broadening of aims and purposes
- a differentiation into lower and upper secondary
- less emphasis on selection and an easier transition from primary school
- a diversification of school types, programmes and the curriculum

Secondary schools now provide compulsory education for pupils aged 11–16, although a number also provide for 16–19 year olds. There are around 3,500 *maintained* secondary schools (i.e. publicly funded) and also 2,342 privately funded, fee-paying schools, outside the state-maintained system (often, surprisingly, these schools are termed 'Public Schools') (Eurydice 2008). In the main, state-maintained schools are:

- comprehensive – non-selective
- co-educational
- non-denominational

The drive towards comprehensive education and equality of provision for all is, however, incomplete. A small number of schools have retained their 'grammar school' status and still select children based on ability. There are also a small number of single sex schools and schools that have a particular religious character, which, in the main, are either Roman Catholic or Church of England (Inca 2008). The rise of the comprehensive school and the quest for equality of provision brought with it the notion of 'one size fits all', in terms of both schools and curriculum. It is obvious this cannot be the case (see Brighouse 2007) and in 2001, the Labour government, in its reform of comprehensive education, escalated the diversification of secondary education, which Alastair Campbell proclaimed would lead to the 'death of the bog standard comprehensive'. However, as Lord Puttnam suggested, these new types of school 'retained the commitment to the ideal of equality, but reflected the changing needs of society and the economy' (BBC 2001). This diversification has led to the development of a number of different types of schools, increasingly geared towards specialization and increasingly linked to partnerships with businesses and other organizations. They include:

- specialist schools
- city technology colleges
- academies

While there has been a long tradition of diversity of provision with the English education system, the current diversification policy has produced a number of criticisms. In particular, the role of big business and other sponsors such as faith groups in the setting up and running of academies has raised particular concerns. For example, there was considerable furore over Emmanuel College, an academy in Gateshead funded by the Vardey Foundation, which promoted the teaching of biblical creationism alongside evolutionary theory (Branigan 2002).

---

### Activity 5.2

What kinds of issues and concerns might be raised over the establishment of specialist schools and academies? (see Baker 2004).

Do you think it is right for a particular school to focus on one specialist area? What might the implications be for pupils, and also for the other non-specialist subject areas?

---

### Phase 4: Upper secondary

Post-compulsory education is available for students aged 16–19. It is provided in a variety of contexts, including sixth forms attached to many secondary schools, sixth form colleges, further education institutions and tertiary colleges. Although there are no official requirements for entry into post-compulsory education, most institutions require a minimum of 5 GCSE or equivalent qualifications at Grades A*–C (Inca 2008). Post-compulsory education in England is typical of an 'integrated system', in that it offers a mixture of both general and pre-vocational courses (Le Métais 2002).

## The National Curriculum

The Education Reform Act (1988) introduced, for the first time in England, a *National Curriculum* that applies to *all children* of compulsory school age. Since its inception, the National Curriculum has undergone a number of revisions, the most recent resulting in a revised secondary curriculum that came on stream in September 2008. The term curriculum, like so many other concepts in education, is used in a variety of ways and is often confused with the notion of a syllabus, which simply refers to the contents of a taught course. The curriculum, however, is a much broader concept than that, encompassing not only the subjects taught, but what is learnt and how that learning is assessed. Thus the curriculum concerns not only the what, but also the why, where, when and how. Bartlett and Burton suggest that the curriculum is:

> . . . a social construction that sits at the very heart of the education system and gives shape and form to much of what happens in schools. Decisions based upon ideological beliefs are made at every

stage in the development and delivery of any curriculum that determine what kind of knowledge is contained in the curriculum, how it is delivered, assessed and so on. (Bartlett and Burton 2007: 7)

According to the QCA, a school's curriculum consists of:

. . . everything that promotes learners' intellectual, personal, social and physical development. As well as lessons and extracurricular activities, it includes approaches to teaching, learning and assessment, the quality of relationships within school, and the values embodied in the way the school operates. (QCA 2008)

Due to the complexity of its nature, it is useful to consider the curriculum in terms of a 'framework' of provision (after Marsh, 2004: 21 in Bartlett and Burton 2007: 81), which has the following typical components:

- aims and purposes
- content
- approach to learning and teaching
- assessment of learning and evaluation of provision

In the development of the revised secondary curriculum, an extended framework was produced, the so called 'Big Picture' of the curriculum that formulates the curriculum around the answers to the following key questions:

- What are we trying to achieve? – Curriculum aims.
- How do we organize learning? – Curriculum organization.
- How well are we achieving our aims? – Curriculum evaluation.

Although the basic components of the 'Big Picture' are not dissimilar to those articulated by Marsh, it is the more holistic conceptualization of the curriculum that is so striking. We will use the questions that frame the 'Big Picture' as the basis for our consideration of the current English National Curriculum.

## What are we trying to achieve?

According to Brighouse, 'a curriculum should reflect agreed purposes and aims for education based on present and future needs' (2007: 1). (We have already discussed the aims and purposes of education, so you may wish to refer to that section in Chapter 2.) Since its establishment, the main purpose of the National Curriculum has been to establish an entitlement to the same broad-based and balanced curriculum for all children, in order to develop them as learners and prepare them for adult life. Another purpose of the National Curriculum is to ensure that standards are comparable in all schools, and that children are provided with a coherent educational experience so that if they move school, they are guaranteed continuity. The establishment of a National Curriculum also sought to facilitate a greater public understanding of what goes on in schools (DES 1989). The National

Curriculum did not have any aims until its revision in 2000, and as White points out, these aims are mainly personal aims and are 'chiefly about the sort of person that school learning is meant to foster – someone who values personal relationships, is a responsible and caring citizen, is entrepreneurial, able to manage risk and committed to sustainable development' (2007: 1).

The original aims and purposes of the National Curriculum have been the subject of considerable criticism. Brighouse (2007: 1), for example, suggests that the 'purpose, scale, framework and choices (of the curriculum) were inappropriate'. He also points out that 'one curriculum does not fit all' and that the curriculum is over-prescriptive, unbalanced, with a limited range of subjects, a flawed assessment design and that it fails to provide a 'seamless' experience if children move schools. Similarly, White suggests that the 'new, whole-person aims', when introduced in 2000, clashed with what he describes as the 'introverted aims of most of the school subjects' (2007: 1).

These perceived flaws and criticisms have led to the development of a new secondary education curriculum, 'a curriculum for the future', which has been 'aims driven'. However, as White (2008) points out, the fact that the National Curriculum subjects have been 'fixed points' and remain unchanged, has placed a huge constraint on the development of the new curriculum. Although the new curriculum is extremely flexible and permits schools to build their own curriculum, responsive to local needs and contexts, the curriculum aims and subjects, together with the five ECM outcomes, pervade what the schools set out to achieve. The aims, purposes and values that underpin the new secondary curriculum are detailed in Table 5.2. Currently, these new aims only apply to the secondary phase, however the primary curriculum is under review and it is highly likely that these will become the aims of the revised primary curriculum.

### How do we organize learning?
The curriculum is organized around four Key Stages (refer to Table 5.1 for more details).

| | | |
|---|---|---|
| Key Stage 1: | ages 5–7 | Years 1–2 |
| Key Stage 2: | ages 7–11 | Years 3–6 |
| Key Stage 3: | ages 11–14 | Years 7–9 |
| Key Stage 4: | ages 14–16 | Years 10–11 |

At each Key Stage, pupils must study a number of subjects, and the details of what is to be taught in each subject at each Key Stage are detailed in the relevant 'Programmes of Study'.

### Phase 1: Early Years Foundation Stage
In 2008, the Early Years Foundation Stage (EYFS) was introduced. The aim was to bring together, under one umbrella, a number of initiatives directed at pre-school children, aged from birth to 5, commensurate with the government's stated commitment to integrate early years education, pre-school childcare and out of school care (Eurydice

**Table 5.2.** What We Are Trying To Achieve? – The Values, Aims and Purposes of the Secondary National Curriculum

| Values | Purposes | Aims | Every Child Matters Outcomes |
|---|---|---|---|
| Education should reflect the enduring values that contribute to personal development and equality of opportunity for all, a healthy and just democracy, a productive economy, and sustainable development. These include values relating to:<br><br>• the self<br>• relationships<br>• the diversity in our society<br>• the environment.<br><br>At the same time, education must enable us to respond positively to the opportunities and challenges of the rapidly changing world in which we live and work. In particular, we need to be prepared to engage as individuals, parents, workers and citizens with economic, social and cultural change, including the continued globalisation of the economy and society, with new work and leisure patterns and with the rapid expansion of communications technologies. | The Education Act (2002) requires that all maintained schools provide a balanced and broadly based curriculum that:<br><br>• promotes the spiritual, moral, cultural, mental and physical development of learners at the school and within society<br>• prepares learners at the school for the opportunities, responsibilities and experiences of adult life.<br><br>The purpose of having a statutory core to the curriculum is:<br><br>• to establish an entitlement.<br>• to establish standards.<br>• to promote continuity and coherence.<br>• to promote public understanding. | The curriculum should enable all young people to become:<br><br>• Successful Learners who enjoy learning, make progress and achieve<br>• Confident Individuals who are able to live safe, healthy and fulfilling lives<br>• Responsible Citizens who make a positive contribution to society. | The Government's aim is for every child, whatever their background or their circumstances, to have the support they need to:<br><br>• Be healthy<br>• Stay safe<br>• Enjoy and achieve<br>• Make a positive contribution<br>• Achieve economic well-being |

Taken From: The Web Pages of National Curriculum: http://curriculum.qca.org.uk/key-stage-3-and-4/ and Every Child Matters: www.everychildmatters.gov.uk/aims

2007/8). Thus the EYFS brought together the 'Curriculum Guidance for the Foundation Stage' (2000), the 'Birth to Three Matters' (2002) framework and the 'National Standards for Under 8s Daycare and Childminding' (2003). White (2008) suggests that a resurgence of the 'developmental approach', first introduced into primary education during the Haddow-Plowden period, can be seen in the new EYFS provision. The EYFS is central to the government's ten year childcare strategy, which was laid down in their policy paper 'Choice for Parents, the Best Start for Children: A Ten Year Strategy for Childcare' (DfES et al. 2004) and the Children's Act (2004). The EYFS aims to ensure that the five ECM outcomes are achieved for children in this age group through 'a coherent and flexible approach to care and learning' (EYFS 2008). All early years practitioners are, therefore, guided in the development of their provision by the early year principles, which are to foster:

- a unique child
- positive relationships
- enabling environments
- learning and development

Educational programmes that are established for children within this age group are focused on learning from play, active learning and develping creativity and critical thinking. Such programmes also have to meet the EYFS goals relating to children's:

- personal, social and emotional development
- communication, language and literacy
- problem solving, reasoning and numeracy
- knowledge and understanding of the world
- physical development
- creative development

(DCSF 2008)

### Phase 2: Primary education – Key Stages 1 and 2

At Key Stages 1 and 2, all pupils study English, Maths, Science and Information and Communications Technology (ICT), Art and Design, Design and Technology, Geography, History, Music and Physical Education and Science. Religious education must also be provided, but parents reserve the right to withdraw their children from religious education if they wish. Schools are also encouraged to provide PSHE, sex education, citizenship and a modern foreign language. In addition to the curriculum guidance, the Primary National Strategy is designed to help schools deliver the National Curriculum more effectively. The strategy contains the 'Primary Framework for Literacy and Numeracy', which provides a number of approaches to improving the quality of provision in those subjects, including, for example, the teaching of phonics (QCA 2008).

Despite the diversity (albeit limited) of the primary curriculum subjects, the findings from research into children's views about the Primary Curriculum suggest that children believe Key Stage 1 is dominated by the study of English and Key Stage 2 by Maths. Pupils also felt that the curriculum was subject-based, focused on the core subjects and mainly determined by the teacher. In the main, girls showed a greater preference than boys for English, while boys had a greater preference for Maths. However, there were no significant trends in gender related subject preferences across the two Key Stages (Robinson and Fielding 2008 plus references).

### Phase 3: Lower secondary – Key Stages 3 and 4

From 2008, at *Key Stage 3* all pupils must study the following subjects: English, Maths, Science, ICT, Art and Design, Citizenship, Modern Foreign Languages, Music and Physical Education. Careers and Sex Education and Religious Education are also statutory subjects. In addition there are non-statutory programmes of study for Personal Wellbeing (including Sex and Relationships, and Drugs education) and Economic Wellbeing and Financial Capability (including Careers Education) (QCA 2008).

At *Key Stage 4*, in addition to English, Maths, Science, ICT, Citizenship and Physical Education, the teaching of Careers Education, Sex Education, Work-Related Learning and Religious Education are also statutory. Pupils also follow a programme of study in a subject from each of the following four *entitlement* areas:

- arts (Art, Music, Dance, Drama, Media Arts)
- design and technology
- humanities (History and Geography)
- modern foreign languages

### Phase 4: Upper secondary 16–18

The National Curriculum does not apply to post-16 education, and so there are no compulsory subjects, except Religious Education. The curriculum at this stage is therefore dependent on the choice of qualifications or subjects that students wish to follow. The nature and range of qualifications available to this age group have been the subject of considerable ongoing debate, with considerable criticism being aimed at the narrowness of the traditional A level programme. With more students being encouraged to stay on in education beyond 16, there has been both a desire and a need to provide a broader base of qualifications for them to study. Since 2000, all students, therefore, have been encouraged to:

- take up to five subjects, including three at A level
- combine academic study with vocational qualifications
- study key business skills

(Eurydice 2008)

There is now a vast and complicated choice of qualifications for students to choose from with, for example, up to 16,000 different vocational qualifications on offer (mainly in FE colleges) (ibid.).

### 14–19 education

The education of 14–19 year olds is now viewed as a continuum, in order to facilitate the transition from secondary education into further study or the world of work. Since 2002, many initiatives have been instigated (14–19: Extending Opportunities, Raising Standards (DfES 2002); 14–19: Opportunity and Excellence (DfES 2003); the Tomlinson Report (2004); the White Paper 14–19: Education and Skills (GB Parliament 2005) and the Education and Skills Bill (2006)) all aimed at raising standards, extending opportunities and providing new qualifications while also encouraging young people to stay on in education beyond the age of 16 (including financial support for students from low income backgrounds) (Eurydice 2008). These initiatives also place a greater emphasis on individualized learning and choice and flexibility in the curricula pathways that provide for both academic and vocational and work-based learning opportunities (DfEE 2001).

### How well are the aims being achieved?

No one can deny that schools and other educational institutions need to be accountable for what goes on within their walls. Teachers, as professionals, have always viewed themselves as accountable for the delivery of the curriculum and the maintenance of standards and of their own and their pupils' behaviour. However, increases in government spending and control over education have led to a greater emphasis on school accountability and resulted in the emergence of a so-called 'audit culture' (Perry and McWilliam 2007). School performance has been reified into a measurable entity based on pupils' achievement in national SATs tests and examinations like GCSEs and A levels. As a consequence, schools can be ranked on the basis of their performance in such tests and *school league tables* can be used to compare schools.

> (This) has led many schools to concentrate their efforts on preparing students for these standardised tests to the relative exclusion of other educational objectives. Such an approach reflects Goodhart's Law: 'What's counted counts', and has led may schools to a reductionist view of education, one defined in terms of scores, market appeal and conformity . . . (Perry and McWilliam 2007: 36)

The development of the new secondary national curriculum has, as we saw earlier, placed a greater emphasis on aims. As a consequence, the accountability measures for schools have also changed. While assessment and improvement in standards are still key measures of performance, other factors, such as levels of attendance and behaviour, civic participation, healthy lifestyle choices and involvement in further study, employment or training, also now come into play. In assessing, therefore, how well the aims of the curriculum have been met, the evaluation procedures focus on the 'whole child' and use a range of measurements rather than just assessment outcomes. The impact of the provision on a wide range of stake-holders, not only the learner, but also parents and the wider community, is also considered (QCA 2008). How well such an approach will marry with the current focus on assessment outcomes is difficult to predict:

> The most radical difference from the 1999 aims is that the 2007 ones are to be made statutory. This is the first time that English schools have had a detailed set of statutory aims to help them shape their curricula. The impact of this change on how twenty-first-century schools, not least primary schools, will operate is potentially profound. It should mean that a school's success is to be judged not primarily in terms of test and exam results but by how far it meets the person-centred requirements embodied in the aims. There are big implications here about how a school's work can be best evaluated and inspected. (White 2008: 12)

### Assessment and National Qualifications

According to Bartlett and Burton (2007), the shape of the National Curriculum was to some extent determined by its assessment framework. The assessment framework consists of a series of *attainment targets* for each subject that set out the 'knowledge, skills and understanding which pupils of different abilities and maturities are expected to have by the end of each key stage' (Education Act 1996, section 353a). Each attainment target has eight level descriptors of increasing difficulty, together with a Level 9 for exceptional performance. The attainment targets indicate the kinds of progress a pupil should make as they work through the key stages, and recognize that pupils do not all progress at the same rate. The majority of pupils are expected to work at:

- levels 1–3 in Key Stage 1 and attain level 2 at the end of the Key Stage
- levels 2–5 in Key Stage 2 and attain level 4 at the end of the Key Stage
- levels 3–7 in Key Stage 3 and attain level 5/6 at the end of the Key Stage

(Eurydice 2008)

At Key Stage 4 and beyond there is a vast array of National Qualifications for students to choose from. Although the qualifications at each level are broadly comparable in terms of the standard of learning, they vary in terms of the purpose, content and duration of the courses to which they apply. A framework of some of the current academic and vocational orientated qualifications is highlighted in Table 5.3, although a new qualifications framework is being prepared.

# Micro-organization: Teaching and learning

Prior to the National Curriculum, how to teach and how to promote learning had generally been left to teachers. The advent of the National Curriculum in 1988 was the dawn of a new era in which teachers' autonomy was gradually reduced. Despite retaining some control over how learning takes place within their classrooms, teachers have been increasingly

**Table 5.3.** Qualifications

|  | Educational Qualifications | Work Related & General Vocational Qualifications |
|---|---|---|
| **Entry Level** | National Curriculum Levels 1, 2 and 3 | |
| **Level 1** | GCSE Grades D–G | NVQ Level 1 |
| **Level 2** | GCSE Grades A*–C | Vocational GCSE  Grades A–C NVQ Level 2  Apprenticeship |
| **Level 3** | AS & A2 level | AS/A2 in Applied Subjects |
|  | AS+A2 = Full A level | NVQ Level 3 Advanced Apprenticeship |
| **Level 4** | Certificate of Higher Education | NVQ Level 4 |
| **Level 5** | Diploma of Higher Education Foundation Degree | NVQ Level 4 |
| **Level 6** | Graduate Certificates & Diplomas Honours Degree | NVQ Level 4 |
| **Level 7** | Postgraduate Certificates & Diplomas Masters Degree | NVQ Level 5 |
| **Level 8** | Doctorate Ph.D | NVQ Level 5 |

*Source*: Based on information available on the QCA and QAA websites

pressured into not only covering all aspects of the curriculum, but having to 'teach to the test' in order to ensure high assessment scores, which has resulted in a 'narrowing of the range of pedagogic methods teachers could employ and to some extent stifled the creativity of both teachers and pupils' (Bartlett and Burton 2007: 91). Such findings are backed up by the views expressed by primary school children, many of whom, according to Robinson and Fielding (2008), feel that almost all of their learning is focused on SATs and that, when teaching, their teachers seem primarily concerned with the outcomes of the tests.

The revised secondary curriculum, however, is conceived as an 'entire learning experience'. The focus is on the learner, on personalized learning, integral assessment and a variety of approaches to learning, both inside and outside the classroom (QCA 2008). This presents a new challenge to teachers, and hopefully, together with the changing emphasis of evaluation and inspection, will result in more creative and dynamic learning environments in the future.

## Activity 5.3

Continue with your reflections on your school experience:

- Compare your experience of primary schooling with your later experiences of education.
- How much choice and flexibility was there in what you learnt and how you were taught?
- Were you aware of what your teachers were trying to achieve? Did they make learning enjoyable, for example, or was the focus on test scores or getting a job?

# Summary

In essence, this chapter has provided an overview of the current structure, aims and purposes of the education system in England. It is only a snapshot, and as we have seen, since 1988 there has been a huge raft of legislation and initiatives that have impacted on the nature and structure of the provision. There is no doubt that changes in legislation and new initiatives will continue to inform the system, as will changes in political ideology and the need for the system to be responsive to both local economic and social imperatives and the impact of globalization. The development of the 'Big Picture' for secondary education and the current review of primary education give some pointers as to how the system will develop in the near future.

## Key references

Bartlett, S. and Burton, D. (2007), *Introduction to Education Studies* (second edition). London: Sage.
Brisard, E. and Menter, I. (2008), 'Compulsory education in the United Kingdom' in Matheson, D. (ed) *An Introduction to the Study of Education* (third edition). Oxford: Routledge.

## Useful websites

www.eurydice.org/portal/page/portal/Eurydice/ByCountryResults?countryCode=UN
　　Eurydice information on the English, Welsh and Irish education systems
www.dcsf.gov.uk
　　The Department for Children, Schools and Families (DCSF) website
www.dius.gov.uk
　　The Department for Innovation, Universities and Skills (DIUS) website
www.qca.org.uk
　　The Qualifications and Curriculum Authority website
www.ofsted.gov.uk
　　The 'New' Ofsted – the Office for Standards in Education, Children's Services and Skills website
http://curriculum.qca.org.uk
　　The National Curriculum website

# Part Three
## Perspectives on Education

# Sociological Perspectives on Education 6

## Sociological perspectives on education

Sociologists of education seek to explain how educational systems function within society. They adopt a variety of theoretical perspectives or approaches that focus on 'the processes of educational transmission' (Ball 2004: 4) and can be grouped into various types. The main groupings we will consider briefly in this chapter are:

- Functionalism
- Marxism and neo-Marxism
- Interactionism
- feminist perspectives
- critical pedagogy

Some of these approaches, such as Functionalism, provide *macro* level explanations of how schools operate within a larger social framework; while other approaches such as Interactionism focus on the *micro* level to explain how individuals within the system inter-relate and interact (Ballantine and Spade 2008).

# Consensus theory: Functionalism

Functionalism dominated sociological theory in the UK until the 1960s and is concerned with the key institutions in society and the large-scale behaviours that develop within those institutions. According to Ballantine and Spade, Functionalist theory is historically important because 'many other theories arose as reactions to or as modifications of functional theory' (2008: 9). Functionalism arose out of the work of Emile Durkheim (ibid.) who put forward the theory that individuals, as part of their behaviour as social beings, need to belong to something that is greater than their immediate environment. He provided a way of viewing schools as part of the mechanism for maintaining social order within society (ibid.). As a theory, Functionalism purports to provide answers to key questions such as, 'What are the functions of education?' and 'How does education contribute to the structures of society?' For example, education can be seen as a socializing agency that is central to the process of transmitting society's norms and values, thus helping to create a consensus regarding the nature of those values. Learning to obey school rules can be seen as a prerequisite for understanding the laws of society. Schools play a vital part in this process by, for example, placing emphasis on particular aspects of 'British culture' within the curriculum, such as the insistence on classical writers in the 1988 English National Curriculum. Schools thus help to socialize children and prepare them for their roles as adult citizens. Functionalists, therefore, perceive society to be a harmonious entity.

According to Ballantine and Spade (2008: 10), from a Functionalist perspective, schools perform the following major 'functions' within society:

- socialization
- selection and training
- promoting change and innovation
- unintended or latent functions – keeping children off the street, child minding, a place for developing youth culture

There is an assumption by functionalists, however, that schools apply standards equally to all pupils and that children are rewarded for their academic achievement. However, this assumption does not take into account the increasingly diverse nature of society and that some values may, therefore, not be universally shared.

# Conflict theory: Marxism and neo-Marxism

## Marxism

Conflict theories arose out of the work of Karl Marx and later, Max Weber, and with respect to education, 'challenge functionalist assumptions that schools are ideologically and politically neutral' (Ballantine and Spade 2008: 12). They argue that the ruling classes use theory and ideology to justify their own position and, therefore, maintain the status quo. It is possible to see educational processes as being central to current methods of social control, as the Church has become less influential in twenty-first century life. People are taught to accept their social position as inevitable within the context of a capitalist ideology. A Marxist perspective on the role of education is, therefore, that schools simply prepare pupils for their fixed place in society, helping to reproduce a stratified workforce that legitimates the position of those in the most influential professions through the use of educational qualifications.

Bowles and Gintis (1976), particularly, emphasized the correspondence between the social relations of the classroom and those of the workplace, where similar hierarchies are in evidence. They were particularly interested in the notion of the 'hidden curriculum', a term that was coined to indicate that there are many things children learn while at school that go beyond the formal curriculum and that would not be included in the stated aims of the institution. For example, rules and obedient behaviour are encouraged, preparing the child to be a passive employee who knows when and to whom they are allowed to speak. A child who ignores these rules can acquire a negative label and suffer the consequences. Furthermore, the purpose of the hidden curriculum may be to persuade children that the inequality they experience is totally justified and unchangeable. Pupils, therefore, have relatively little power, while critical thinking and creativity are positively discouraged. Marxists would regard the notion that schools offer equal opportunities for all as a myth disguising the reality that schools actually reproduce inequality, and attribute failure, and therefore, poverty, to lack of individual effort.

The work of Paul Willis in his famous publication *Learning to Labour* (1979) offered a counter-argument in his detailed study of working class 'lads' who felt powerful enough to reject the culture of their school and replace it with their own sub-culture. There was indeed a correspondence in the way they viewed both school and work, but the boys were not seduced by the idea that hard work necessarily resulted in acknowledgement and reward, and subsequently created their own lives and identity based on their own values. Willis's study remains an influential piece of research, despite criticisms of its very small scale.

## Neo-Marxism

One of the most influential thinkers with regard to the way social relations are interpreted is the French philosopher Pierre Bourdieu (Ball 2004). Bourdieu explains the assets individuals accumulate during their lives in economic terms, with the following three categories being most significant:

> **Economic capital**, which can be immediately converted into money, for example property.
> **Cultural capital**, which can be turned into economic capital and is institutionalized in material things such as educational qualifications. This particular concept has been extremely helpful when

considering the ways in which certain social groups continue to succeed within the education system while others do not.

**Social capital**, which consists of such assets as social connections, which can be institutionalized in such phenomena as the nobility, for example. This theory can help to explain unequal educational achievement among children coming from different social classes, which in economic terms relates to the profits and losses of the educational market.

*Cultural capital* is an important concept in education, and can exist as qualities of both mind and body. It can also be objectified in the form of cultural 'goods', for example pictures, books, instruments and also in educational qualifications. Accumulating cultural capital requires time and money in the form of years of study. It also involves working on the self, consciously striving for personal improvement, which requires effort as well. It stands to reason then that those who are born into materially better circumstances are able to acquire the necessary capital more quickly, as others may need to work to support themselves during this period, or in the case of children, wait while their parents try to earn the necessary funds. Qualifications are the symbols of this acquired capital, and their value increases as they become more exclusive (which is a controversial aspect of the current drive to increase numbers in higher education).

*Social capital*, on the other hand, comes from belonging to a powerful group, a class, a family, a tribe, the more prestigious the connections the group has, the more capital the individual can accumulate. We can see here how marriage can be used as a way of connecting powerful groups, and as such, became so central to many great stories, particularly in the nineteenth century. Social capital can be paraded in a ritualistic manner at occasions such as parties, hunt balls, race meetings and so on. Places can also indicate the degree of social capital a person has in relation to where they live, where 'better' schools are situated, what kind of clubs and leisure facilities are available, where status can constantly be played out and recognition reaffirmed. In fact, the middle class fear of failure has resulted in the phenomenon of families moving house to be within the catchment area of a school with a better reputation.

Bourdieu argues that because of the power that certain classes have within society, their culture is adopted by schools as the most valuable, 'the norm', and therefore children from middle class families start school with an advantage, they will 'fit' into the school more easily in terms of their behaviour, language and attitude (Bourdieu 1977 in Reay 2004). Andy Green (1990) argues that of all countries, England exemplifies the most overt use of the schooling system by one class over another in order to keep people in subordinate positions. Reay, referring to the work of Adam Smith in 1785, goes on to explain that the commitment to working class education by the growing middle class in the early nineteenth century was based, not on altruistic aims of encouraging individual potential, but on a desire to 'contain and pacify rather than to educate and liberate' (2004: 30). In other words, the purpose of encouraging education among the working classes was purely instrumental, not liberal or intrinsic. She also argues that the late nineteenth century school system was established in order to police and control the lower classes – they were to be taught to know their place.

Some would argue that the same principles can still be perceived today. Hatcher, for example, maintains that despite the movement over the past 150 years towards achieving greater educational equality (usually with regard to access), 'the state school system continued, and still continues to serve the middle class much better than it does those of the majority of children from working class backgrounds' and further, 'one in three children are in families that fall below the poverty line', but efforts to address such inequality have been at odds with policies relating to market forces (2004: 130). Moreover, 'those who govern are prisoners of a reassuring entourage of young, white, middle-class technocrats who often know almost nothing about the everyday lives of their fellow citizens and have no occasion to be reminded of their ignorance' (Bourdieu 1993: 627 in Reay 2004: 31). From this perspective, we can see that the main role of education is to reproduce a class system and uphold the dominant culture. Reay (2004) maintains that that the history of working class education has traditionally been a story of failure, while those who break through into academic success see themselves as somehow escaping the predictable limitations of their class (see David Dickinson's autobiography in Chapter 1 for an interesting exploration of these issues).

Do we, in fact, still pathologize working class childhood and attribute occasional successes to the efforts or talents of the individuals concerned? Will widening participation in higher education provide the answer to the seemingly endless cycle of educational disadvantage? Consider that over 80 per cent of pupils with the best GCSE results come from social groups 1 and 2, whatever school they go to (Ryan 2000 in Reay 2004). Consider too for a moment, whether, in your own experience, pupils always received the rewards they deserved according to how hard they worked. Is the education system fair? Does a pupil's gender, ethnicity or class play any part in their educational achievement?

# Interactionism

Interactionism is the name given to a group of perspectives that include phenomenology, symbolic interactionism and ethnographical research methodology. In contrast to functionalists, interactionists place great emphasis on small-scale social interactions between individuals or groups and specific contexts. The focus is on the way people develop understanding of the world through the observation and interpretation of behaviour. This includes both instinctive and conscious behaviour and, with regard to education, how classroom interactions contribute to the social construction of identity. Studies are often at the micro level and focus in detail on how people, and pupils, create their own meaning out of their day-to-day encounters with groups and individuals around them. Bartlett et al. cite Mead as the 'founder of symbolic interactionism' (2002: 172), whose ideas focused particularly on how human beings construct a sense of 'self'.

Interactionism has, in turn, become closely linked to *labelling theory*, through the process by which people, including teachers, categorize phenomena in order to make sense of the world around them. In schools, some teachers may be very quick to assign labels to children, based, possibly, on their interpretation of very few actions. For example, some children quickly come to be seen as trouble-makers and teachers will then interpret that entire pupil's behaviour in the light of such a 'label'. Consider the experience of *Student T* in Chapter 1, and how teachers' defining of children can result in a *self-fulfilling prophecy*. Pupils and teachers negotiate their roles, and these may change quite frequently, meaning that identity is constantly being redefined through social interactions.

A highly influential piece of small-scale research was Basil Bernstein's work on language and culture, based on his experience of teaching in London's East End. Bernstein coined the phrases 'restricted' and 'elaborate codes', relating to the language used by working class and middle class children respectively. A restricted code he saw as a system of short, simple sentences often based on a shared knowledge among close groups, such as families. An elaborate code, in contrast, provides detailed information and explanations using complex sentence structure and is not tied to context. Bernstein argued that middle class children are able to switch easily between both codes, being equally fluent, which gives them an advantage in school and in the workplace. Bernstein makes no judgement on the relative value of such speech patterns, but it is inevitable that one group would come to be seen as having better understanding and being able to communicate with teachers more easily (see Sadovnik 1991). Other researchers, such as Labov (1973), presented such variations in speech as 'different' but not necessarily unequal. The main criticism of Interactionism is that it focuses too closely on detail and the individual. Interactionists do not explain power relations or the nature of social change adequately, but can be linked to post-modernism in that all knowledge is seen as relative and subjective.

# Critical pedagogy

*Critical pedagogy considers how education can provide individuals with the tools to better themselves and strengthen democracy, to create a more egalitarian and just society, and thus to deploy education in a process of progressive social change.*

*(Kellner 2000)*

In his chapter on social class and school, Richard Hatcher concludes with a statement 'that a transformation is required in the educational experience of working class children if we are to transform their prospects' (Hatcher 2005: 145). He calls this approach 'education for emancipation' (ibid.: 143 and 145), one that can be considered to be a 'direction for those in education who still dare to hope' (Darder 1995) and has come to be known as 'critical pedagogy'. At the core of critical pedagogy lies a commitment to democracy and freedom from oppression, arising as it did out of the work of *Paolo Freire*. It has since been expounded by educational thinkers like Apple and Giroux among others. It is a perspective that goes beyond liberal pedagogy, which has come to be seen as reinforcing forms of inequality, because it permits the teacher to become a powerful agent for transformation in the classroom. Shor (1992) identifies the following important goals of critical pedagogy:

- opposing socialization
- transforming society
- practising democracy
- encouraging student participation
- raising awareness of the thoughts and language expressed in daily life
- inviting students to reflect socially on their conditions and to consider overcoming limits

Critical pedagogy, therefore, enables the teacher, at the centre of the constant demands of a bureaucratic nightmare, with assessment, accountability, standardized curricula, to challenge the status quo in the education system and, in turn, empower their students. It takes as a given that society remains unequal along the lines of class, race and gender, and relates to the ideas of Dewey regarding the ways in which schools mould an individual into a certain set of beliefs and ways of behaving. Therefore, schools play their part in perpetuating the 'invisible hegemony' of social control.

Progressive teachers who adopt this critical approach engage in fundamental debates around the purpose of school and the contribution that schools make to the unequal divisions in society. They encourage critical thinking in their students, who, in turn, will fight for democracy and freedom. It is a pedagogy that values the student voice, raises consciousness, respects the needs of the student and helps them to become participants in society. It is a pedagogy that has to be based on trust (Corrigan and Chapman 2008), while allowing an 'interpersonal space' to be created in the classroom, 'where knowledge is generated and identities negotiated through collaborative relations of power' (Cummins 2003 in Cumming and Kent 2008: 3). Criticisms of critical pedagogy include the ironic notion that, by encouraging students to adopt this perspective, teachers are, in fact imposing their own views.

---

### Activity 6.1

Consider your own experience of school. Were there any occasions when students' opinions were listened to?

Do you recognize any aspects of critical pedagogy in your teachers' approaches?

How far do you agree that this form of teaching and learning will transform society?

# Perspectives on race and gender

## Gender

How can schools create more equal life chances in relation to race and gender? In the 1970s and 1980s, there was a lot of interest in how the social processes of education led to discrimination on the basis of gender. If children learn their social roles from school as well as home, this is likely to include gendered behaviour. In the primary curriculum, stereotyping was often seen in reading schemes and lesson content that emphasized the different positions of men and women in society. In secondary schools, girls were often encouraged to select for stereotyped options and careers. Girls were also marginalized in the classroom and playground, and studies of interaction would usually reveal that teachers spent far more time with boys (see Oakley 1975; Spender 1982 and Whyte 1983).

The movement that has sought to ask questions about gender equality in public life has been called *feminism*. Liberal feminists favoured reforms that could be brought about democratically while radical feminists advocated more dramatic change, a 'sexual revolution'. 'Patriarchy', meaning the rule of the fathers, is a term coined to express the structures in society that keep women oppressed.

Over the past 20 years, as girls' assessment results began to steadily improve, attention has moved to the growing concern with boys' underachievement within the education system, and a debate has developed around the relationship between education and masculinity. This has been accompanied by an increasing awareness that particular minority ethnic groups also fare less well in terms of academic success. According to Rhamie:

> In 2006, the government published statistics showing the ethnic breakdown of all groups of pupils taking GCSE exams in 2005. The results revealed that Black Caribbeans performed poorly compared to all other ethnic groups with only 41.7% achieving 5 GCSEs at A* to C grades. This compared to 48.4% for Pakistani pupils, 52.7% for Bangladeshi pupils; both traditionally low performing groups and 55.1% for White pupils. The only exception was Traveller of Irish heritage (22.5%) and Gypsy/Roma (14.7%) but the numbers of pupils in these groups were very small. (DFES 2006 in Rhami 2006: 2)

It is interesting to note, however, that there have been no press headlines congratulating girls on their success! Shortly before Labour came to power in 1997, Tony Blair made his infamous public commitment to education as being synonymous with social justice, liberty and opportunity. However, in the face of growing concern over educational standards, this commitment was hastily replaced with an insistence on the part of Estelle Morris, the then Secretary of State for Education, that performance league tables were the key to focusing attention where it was needed. Since then, the government has continued to use educational attainment as the main criterion for judging progress in terms of equality. This focus ignores the cultural and social factors that contribute to the ongoing failure of certain social groups, by placing the emphasis firmly on under-achievement. One of the problems with this approach is that, too often, the problem is located within 'the other', that is, lack of success is attributed to the individual's lack of effort.

If, however, we take on board the idea that the concept of 'difference' is socially constructed, then we should incline towards the position put forward by Gillborn and Youdell that 'groups defined socially by class, gender, race, ethnicity and sexuality are inherently no less capable of educational participation and success' (Gillborn and Youdell 2000: 4). Otherwise, we are being drawn into the liberal argument that differences in attainment are the natural result of a meritocracy. However:

> . . . the widespread media attention given to the underachievement of boys has failed to address . . . the real issue that it is pupils from ethnic minority backgrounds who, along with those from the working class, experience the most pronounced inequalities in our education system. Inequalities which have become more apparent as schools move towards an 'A–C economy' in an effort to secure favourable league table positions. (Smith 2003: 287)

### *What are the reasons boys are falling behind girls?*

There are no definitive answers to this question. Possible reasons include the changing patterns of male employment; many traditionally 'male' jobs have disappeared from the UK. The demands of an academic curriculum may be at odds with boys' needs to play out their masculinity in front of their peers. There are also factors around gendered preferences with respect to curriculum content and assessment procedures. We are also, of course, seeing achievement only in terms of performance data, and while it remains true that girls are now doing better than boys at every assessment stage, the gender imbalance in influential occupations remains in favour of men.

## Race

With regard to race, black pupils continue to be excluded from school in disproportionate numbers and, despite steady progress, remain behind their white peers in the race for qualifications. The response has been a long list of initiatives such as homework clubs, black gospel choirs, programmes to get fathers more involved with their sons, mentoring schemes and so on (Smith 2003: 283), some of which have had considerable success. However, the question remains, why are such phenomena as supplementary schools necessary? As Sonia Nieto states:

> Failure to learn does not develop out of thin air; it is scrupulously created through policies, practices, attitudes and beliefs. In a very concrete sense, the results of educational inequality explain by example what a society believes its young people are capable of achieving and what they deserve. (Nieto 1999: 175)

## Case study: On the margins

Within the context of widening participation to higher education, a few of us working on teacher education courses in a North West University have noticed a pattern of failure among a group of Irish young men, usually working class, first generation students. Some of these young men bring with them a history of disaffection from the school system, yet feel a strong sense of vocation. Having come to live in another country at the age of eighteen, they can find themselves on the margins of the university experience; and their issues of culture, language, religion and class we felt were worthy of exploration.

The perception that the Irish students were different was held by a number of people, both English and Irish, and there were sometimes clashes between middle clash English students and some younger, more boisterous students, many of whom were Irish. The latter group maintained that they felt like 'outsiders' in relation to the main university community. The following is part of the data collected from one interviewee, who is referred to as Anthony.

Anthony came to the programme leader's attention when she had to reprimand him about his behaviour. He had earned the reputation among staff of being an aggressive young man of whom a number of other students were afraid. The programme leader's initial impression was of someone who was quick-witted with a lively sense of humour, who went on to show an interest in the exploration of classism within education.

Anthony was a working class Catholic from the Republic of Ireland. He was the first person in his family to continue in education and attend university. In fact, he had made a conscious decision to leave all his peers behind in order to pursue his educational aspirations.

> I got my results back and all the lads were there. It was one weekend we got our results back and we were all in the pub and I was saying, 'You know what, there's no way that I'm going to sit here and go to this pub every day of the week, every weekend same thing, week in and out . . . I'm getting out of here'. So all of them went off and got jobs in factories and done carpentry and I said 'I can't be a**** with this, I want to be a PE teacher. I want to do something with my life. I want to change. I don't want to be sat in W. for the rest of my life'. So I made the decision to go back to school and repeat my leaving certificate.

As with other interviewees, Anthony regarded himself as not particularly successful in school, explaining that the teachers had only been interested in those at the top of the A-stream. He was given encouragement by only two teachers, and consequently enjoyed their subjects and chose to study them at university. It was the PE teacher's suggestion that he might consider becoming a PE teacher himself. According to Govindarajan, 'when a student feels that the instructor has a sincere interest in the student's welfare and viewpoints an excellent catalyst is provided for higher education performance' (in Corrigan and Chapman 2008: 2). His parents were very supportive, and Anthony suspects that his father was to some extent living out a life through him he would have liked for himself. In reality, both Anthony's father and brother had been excluded from school at an early age.

Anthony recalled two further incidents that had been significant in his educational journey. In primary school, he and a number of boys from the same council estate had been selected to have extra lessons at lunchtime on how to speak properly. The lessons only continued for a short time as the boys couldn't stop laughing at the strange way the elocution teacher spoke. This has obvious resonance with the work of both Bernstein and Labov discussed earlier in this chapter. The boys' language code was deemed to be inferior by the school, yet they were secure enough in their own identity to be able to resist and subvert the crude attempt to make them fit into the dominant culture. Later, a mere accident of educational administration, the fact that there were too few pupils to make up an additional B-stream set, led to Anthony being placed in the bottom set of the A-stream. Anthony was convinced that had he stayed in the B-steam, he would

⇨

never have found his way to university, based on the fact that none of the boys in that group had stayed on at school beyond the age of 16. The outcome of this 'accident' illustrates the power of labels that often follow pupils throughout their school-life. As it was, Anthony was able to renegotiate his school identity, and through that, his life-chances were considerably improved.

Anthony was able to draw on his own experiences of school in developing empathy with some of the more disaffected children he encountered on his school placements. As Grinter (2000) points out so aptly, a key aspect of teachers' understanding of inequality needs to be accompanied by an awareness of the role that schools and teachers play in that process. Grinter (2000) also identifies that the experience of inequality can result in the lowering of personal expectations and an acceptance of an assigned status, something that Anthony avoided, yet his school-friends did not.

The above extract illustrates that, contrary to some research (see Lynch and O'Riorden 1997), working class parents, while not necessarily having succeeded within the education system themselves, can be instrumental in their children's application to further and higher education. It also provides evidence of the continuing power of teachers to 'both open and close doors' (Lynch and O'Riorden 1999: 127), and the significance of the issue of identity, and the ways in which this is socially constructed.

*This is an extract, written by Sue Lewis and taken from an unpublished paper presented at the CARN Conference in 2003 by Sue Lewis, Paul Bowen, Angela Harnett and Sheila Anthony.*

It is possible to analyse key phases of educational development in the UK from the perspective of equal opportunities, starting with comprehensivization and the raising of the school leaving age in the 1970s, through the abandoning of a two-tier examination system in the 1980s, to the cross-curricular dimensions articulated in the 1988 Education Reform Act and recent initiatives such as 'Excellence in Cities'. None of these has succeeded in eradicating inequality. There is also the relatively unexplored issue of the negative experience of education suffered by an increasingly vocal minority group, those students who are lesbian, gay or bi-sexual.

# Summary

This chapter has provided a brief overview of the sociological theories that are used to explore significant influences and issues in education. Functionalist and Conflict approaches offer useful analyses of social phenomena, while Interactionist theories consider the more detailed relationships that occur on a day-to-day basis in the classroom. Such approaches also help to provide an understanding of the origins and effects of the inequality that persists within the education system. Yet despite the gloomy messages some optimism remains.

> If teachers begin by challenging societal inequities that inevitably place some students at a disadvantage; if they struggle against institutional policies that are unjust; if they undergo a process of personal transformation . . . and, finally, if they engage with colleagues in a collaborative encounter to transform their own practices to achieve high quality education for all students, then the outcome is sure to be more positive. (Nieto 1999: 175)

## Key references

Ballantine, J. H. and Spade, J. Z. (eds) (2008), *Schools and Society. A Sociological Approach to Education* (third edition). Los Angeles: Pine Forge Press.

Ball, S. J. (ed) (2004), *The Routledge Falmer Reader in Sociology of Education*. London: Routledge Falmer.

## Useful websites

www.sociology.org.uk
 Sociology Central – for useful student-friendly resources on all aspects of sociology

# Philosophical and Ideological Perspectives

## Philosophy and education

The word 'philosophy' comes from Greek, and literally means 'the love of wisdom'. Philosophers engage in 'reasoned argument' in their search for the meaning of concepts and a clarification of questions about such things as human nature, knowledge, morality, ethics and truth. Philosophers of education, therefore, ask fundamental questions of education (see earlier chapters) such as:

- What is education for, what are its aims and purposes?
- Who should be educated?
- How should they be educated?

These questions are, according to Noddings (2007), perennial questions and the answers to them change with time and context.

There are a number of approaches used by philosophers in order to elicit meaning, although any in-depth consideration of these approaches is beyond the scope of this text (for a more detailed account see Noddings 2007). The following are some of those approaches:

**Analytical philosophy**, which has its origins in the ideas of Bertrand Russell (1872–1969) who believed that reality could be 'analysed' and broken down into basic elements and relationships. Today, analytical philosophers concentrate on an analysis of the meaning of words and concepts in the various contexts they are used in order, for example to clarify our understanding of such terms as education and teaching.

**Existensialism** is concerned with the individual and how the individual defines him- of herself (ibid.: 62). It considers individuals' intentions or reasons why they choose to do something or communicate something. In a way it is concerned with individuals being more self-aware and taking responsibility for their own actions.

**Phenomenology** is concerned with describing 'how we are' (ibid.: 71). It is an attempt to describe our mental state or consciousness.

**Critical theory** considers the social causes and consequences of various forms of domination in society, be it as a consequence of class, race or gender. Critical theorists suggest that by providing all students with so called 'privileged knowledge', such domination can be broken down (ibid.: 75).

**Epistomology** is a large area of philosophy that is concerned with asking questions about the theory of knowledge and what, for example, we mean by truth.

**Post-modernism**, according to Burke, denies 'human thought the ability to arrive at any objective account of reality' (2000: 3). While accepting 'local truths' like scientific knowledge and mathematical principles, post-modernists reject the notion of an absolute truth or an 'all encompassing description of knowledge' (Noddings 2007: 78).

According to Noddings (2007: 81) it is analytical philosophy and critical thinking that have had the greatest impact on educational thinking. Analytical philosophy, for example, has contributed greatly to our understanding of the concept of education and what it means to be educated (see Chapters 2 and 3), while critical theory has made significant contributions to our understanding of issues of race, class and gender with respect to educational attainment (see Chapter 6). If we now reconsider the three fundamental questions we highlighted earlier, philosophy has helped us gain a consensus understanding of what education is and what its main aims and purpose are. We are also currently in agreement that, in principle, everyone has a right to an education. However, as Noddings highlights, 'our great debate is over *how* individual children should be educated, and the debate today is heated' (2007: 2).

# Ideology and education

The term *ideology* is difficult to define and its useage can vary. However, Apple suggests that:

Most people seem to agree that one can talk about ideology as referring to some sort of 'system' of ideas, beliefs, fundamental commitments, or values about social reality, but here the agreement ends. The interpretations differ according to both the *scope* or range of the phenomena which are presumably ideological and the *function* – what ideologies actually do for the people who 'have' them. (Apple 2004: 18)

Apple also points to three ways in which the term can be used (2004: 18):

- as a justification for the activities of a particular professional group
- with reference to political programme or social movement
- with reference to a particular world view or 'symbolic universe'

From an educational perspective, an ideology can be defined as 'any package of educational ideas held by a group of people about formal arrangements for education' (Matheson 2008: 21). Ideologies work at different levels within an education system, from informing education acts at a national level to influencing classroom practices (ibid.). There have been numerous attempts to describe and group different educational ideologies:

**The dichotomous approach** is the most common approach, which simply contrasts competing viewpoints such as:
    teacher-centred versus child-centred
    traditional versus progressive
**The grouping approach** seeks to categorize ideologies based on the extent to which they emphasize either the individual, society or knowledge (Schrimshaw 1983; Morrison and Ridley 1989, both in Bartlett and Burton 2007: 23).
**The analytical approach**, which seeks to establish the major features of an ideology at either a systems or a classroom level (see Meighan and Harber 2007: 219). One such analytic approach is the *typology* proposed by Meighan and Siraj-Blatchford (2003: 197 in Bartlett and Burton 2007: 26), which suggests that any ideology of education is based on a number of theories that include a theory of:
    - discipline and order
    - knowledge, its content and structure
    - learning and the learner's role
    - teaching and the teacher's role
    - resources appropriate for teaching
    - organization of learning situations
    - assessment that learning has taken place
    - aims, objectives and outcomes
    - parents and parents' role
    - locations appropriate for learning
    - power and its distribution

There are a multitude of ideologies that influence educational thought and practice; however, they 'are not static. They evolve and they may expire' (Matheson 2008: 33). The following are examples of the most commonly articulated educational ideologies (see Barlett and Burton 2007, Matheson 2008 and Meighan and Harber 2007).

- **Elitist and conservative ideologies** are concerned with maintaining the status quo in society. According to Matheson (2008), such an ideology privileges character rather than intellect.
- **Technocratic and rationalizing ideologies** are concerned with the relevancy of education to the labour market.
- **Liberal and egalitarian ideologies** are concerned with notions of social democracy and providing equality of opportunity for all.
- **Romantic and individualistic ideologies** are connected to a child-centred view of education and with progressive education.

---

### Activity 7.1

Are you able to distinguish any of these ideological perspectives in the policies and practices that you encountered during your own education or in our current educational provision?

---

In the next section we will explore the life and work of a number of educational philosophers and thinkers whose ideas about education have influenced and developed a contemporary view of education that is framed by one ideological perspective – the Romantic or individualistic. In this way, it is hoped that the link between philosophical thought and the development of an ideological perspective may become clear. We therefore start the journey with Rousseau, whose ideas and thinking sparked the Romantic tradition in education.

# Educationalists in the Romantic tradition: Rousseau (1712–1778)

Born in France, Rousseau was a Romantic philosopher who believed that human beings are essentially 'good' and that they possess a natural curiosity about the world. His view of education was that it should develop the child artistically and emotionally to produce a creative and compassionate individual. According to Novello, many writers refer to Rousseau as 'the leading inspirational force behind the establishment of progressive education' (1999: 2). Some of Rousseau's followers tried to put his ideas into practice, using their own interpretations of his ideas; these included Pestalozzi, Froebel and Dewey, who introduced Rousseau's work to the United States. Common to all these educational philosophers was the notion of 'child-centred pedagogy' (Novello 1999: 5).

## Childhood as a separate state

Rousseau was, possibly, the first person to formulate the idea that childhood is a separate and precious state, not simply adulthood in miniature. As such, we can see that Rousseau is the precursor to all our discussions around childhood and children's well-being. Many in the 'progressive tradition' believed that the child should be free to select their own activities and develop naturally. However, contrary to this, Novello (1999) argues that there is another aspect of Rousseau's theory, which was that the child would 'naturally' choose only those activities that the teacher would think appropriate, having been guided towards those. The teacher would, therefore, be subtly controlling the child's development at every stage. What if, however, the child did not behave according to the teacher's wishes? This controversial interpretation of Rousseau's philosophy was not emphasized to the same degree by his readers and followers.

## Romanticism

Rousseau's later work focused on his realization that humans could find peace and fulfilment by becoming in tune with the natural world and, out of this, was born the whole Romantic movement, which so dominated writers, thinkers and poets of the late eighteenth and early nineteenth centuries. Humans were thought to be governed by the laws of nature and should, therefore, seek not only to understand their environment, but also to be free from the constraints placed upon them by society. We can see this view emerging in the work of the educators that we will be looking at a little bit later in this chapter. The inner world of the child also became increasingly important, including how this understanding of self could be communicated through such activities as painting and writing. This would be said to be the beginnings of reflexivity as we understand it.

Interestingly, Novello (1999) also observes that Rousseau was the first to propose a national system of education, the purpose of which would be to produce good citizens, albeit of equal standing. This could be said to have influenced the creation of secular state schools in a number of democratic countries such as France and the United States, their aim being to promote literacy and a sense of citizenship among the general population (Cubberley 1920 in Novello 1999).

Rousseau described his ideas about education in his work *Emile*. However, it is clear in the reading of the text that his views about how his male character Emile should be educated vary considerably from his view of his female character, Sophie's, education. According to Noddings, when discussing Emile's education:

> . . . Rousseau's child starts out good. If he . . . is educated properly, he will grow into a free, loving, and responsible adult. He must, in an important sense, be allowed to guide his own education. His teacher should facilitate – provide appropriate objects and potential experiences, anticipate his needs and direction of growth, and abstain from the sort of coercion that spoils almost all children . . . Rousseau's is, in many ways, a lovely view of education. (Noddings 2007: 17)

On the other hand, Rousseau, in describing Sophie's education, condemned women to a domestic role:

> The entire education of women must be relative to men. To please them, to be useful to them, to be loved and honoured by them, to rear them when they are young, to care for them when they

are grown up, to counsel and console, to make their lives pleasant and charming, these are the duties of women at all times, and they should be taught them in their childhood. (Rousseau in Noddings 2007: 17)

Rousseau's main view of the purpose of education was that it should develop the child artistically and emotionally, to produce a creative and compassionate human being. This stemmed from his belief that human beings are naturally 'good', which was in total opposition to the views of many religious groups at the time. As a result, Rousseau was disliked by government and church alike and was forced to flee persecution many times during his lifetime.

---

### Activity 7.2

- Can you relate to Rousseau's ideas?
- Do you think he was correct to emphasize the importance of feelings?
- Can you think of aspects of modern education that Rousseau would agree with?

---

# Johann Heinrich Pestalozzi (1746–1827)

Despite the violent opposition his writing provoked, Rousseau also had many keen followers, one of whom was Johann Heinrich Pestalozzi who was born in Switzerland in 1746. Pestalozzi put Rousseau's theories into practice in the schools he established. He opened the first school in the grounds of his estate, to teach the poor children of his own employees (Novello 1999), and others were opened to cater for orphans of the Napoleonic wars. He believed that the poor could achieve the same as their wealthier counterparts provided they received a good education. Like Rousseau, he believed that human beings possess a natural goodness and are capable of being responsible for their own learning, a very modern concept for the time. Also, like Rousseau, Pestalozzi believed that children should be 'educated through their senses', developing what he termed 'object lessons' that usually ended in a moral (Noddings 2007: 19).

Pestalozzi favoured a caring approach and a curriculum that included a balance of the arts and practical skills, even manual labour (Koetzsch 1997), believing that the intellect develops naturally from a basis of concrete experiences. The children even went on field trips and collected natural objects. In this, and in his rejection of corporal punishment, Pestalozzi was far ahead of his time and his work found its way to the United States where similar methods were being advocated by leading thinkers such as Emerson and Thoreau. This focus on the development of human potential was to be established further by two leading educational philosophers on opposite sides of the world, John Dewey in America and Tsunesaburo Makiguchi in Japan.

# Maria Montessori (1870–1952)

Maria Montessori was born near Ancona in Italy on 31 August 1870. When she was 24, she became the first woman to receive a medical degree from Rome University. However, she became interested in the cognitive development of children with learning difficulties, and returned to university to study education. Having studied the behaviour of children with learning difficulties, Montessori became convinced that they were not uneducable and so developed a system for teaching children with special needs.

In 1907, Montessori opened the first *Casa dei Bambini* (house of children) for disadvantaged children in Rome. Montessori was curious to see whether her methods would be appropriate for children without learning difficulties, but who suffered from social deprivation. Educators across the world were astonished to discover that these children learned to read and write by the age of 5. This led to international fame for Montessori, and schools using her methods opened all over the world.

## Montessori's philosophy

Montessori's philosophy was in the tradition of Rousseau, Pestalozzi and also Froebel, all of whom recognized the innate potential of the child and their ability to develop in an environment of freedom and love. Montessori believed that young children have an innate life force, derived from God, and through this they develop naturally and have a desire to reach their potential. As children are acutely sensitive to their surroundings, these should, therefore, be as pleasant as possible to encourage growth.

Montessori was one of the first to recognize that childhood was a specific state of being and that adults depended on children just as much as children depended on adults. Through her observations of children's behaviour, she came to believe that classroom activities were central to children's construction of their own identities. In her theory of child development, she proposed that young children go through key stages or sensitive periods. These were:

- a need for order in the environment
- the use of the hand and tongue
- the development of walking
- a fascination with minute and detached objects
- a period of intense social interest

There are a number of links to Piaget (Noddings 2007) that we can see here, for example both believed in the role of sensori-motor training and that a child's cognitive development moves through stages from concrete experience to abstract concepts, and that these stages are at fixed points. From birth to 6 are the most crucial years for child development according to Montessori, as it is during these years that children are able to learn most rapidly.

Montessori believed that children possess a natural sense of education directive that does not need reward or punishment to manifest itself. The role of the teacher is, therefore, a very important aspect of her education system. Teachers should not be strict disciplinarians but simply observers who facilitate the child's needs as they see them arising. Teachers must create an appropriate learning environment that supports and stimulates the pupils. This environment is not fixed, however, but can be rearranged according to the learning stage or activity the pupil has selected. Traditional schools that limit a child's opportunity to choose could, in fact, be harmful to children's natural development.

According to Lillard (1972), one of the most important results of Montessori's own observations of children is the 'law of work', where children appear to reach a state of peace and fulfilment after working hard to complete a task that is self-selected. A second principle is that of the drive for independence, a force that should not be impeded by an overly strict teacher. A third principle is that of 'attention', which is the child's ability to concentrate intensely and which is part of the consolidation phase that develops personality (ibid.: 39).

One of the most controversial aspects of Montessori's philosophy was her theory that children also grow into a phase of natural obedience to adults, a view that may have unfortunate connotations for many of us today. However, this form of obedience, according to Montessori, is part of the development of the child's will and she believed that will and obedience are two aspects of the same phenomenon (see Dewey).

There are two key components within Montessori's teaching methods (Lillard 1972: 50). One is the environment, including materials. Another is the teacher. The materials must meet the child's needs and are divided into four categories: daily living; sensorial; artistic and academic. Materials are often concrete, such as wooden shapes, so that the child can explore sensorially before going on to absorb abstract ideas. Colours in the classroom are bold and harmonious.

As stated earlier, the teacher acts as a facilitator in the Montessori classroom and helps to guide the child in order to develop their will and their moral sense. A Montessori teacher's attitude 'could be summed up in one word – respect' (Lillard 1972: ix). The ultimate goal, however, of Montessori's system is self-discipline.

---

### Activity 7.3

- How important do you consider the notion of respect to be between teacher and pupils? Is it something that was evident in your own experience of school?
- Do you think that young children are able to direct their own learning as in a Montessori classroom? Why/why not?

# John Dewey (1859–1952)

John Dewey was largely responsible for the mainstreaming of romanticism within the American education system. Dewey was a central figure in the development of 'secular humanism', later to be known as progressive education (Koetzsch 1997). Dewey attended the University of Vermont and became Head of the Department of Psychology and Pedagogy at Chicago University. In 1904, he became Professor of Philosophy at Columbia University, New York. He rejected the Christianity of his upbringing in favour of a humanist and evolutionist approach. His views were based on the notion that our ideas are derived from concrete experience, not abstract theory; that life is as we see it and feel it. He believed that human beings have infinite potential, although environmental factors have a role to play (here he echoes the views of Makiguchi, the founder of Soka Education in Japan).

Dewey held that the aim of education was 'to help the child develop an interest in the world, to learn, think critically . . . to become an active member of the community' (Koetzsch 1997: 9) and to find his/her place in a democratic world. The desire to learn should be paramount. Through this approach, schools could bring about a transformation of the world. Dewey's proposals for education were radically different from the philosophy of the public school system at the time. His basic principles include the assumptions that:

- children want to learn and only need direction from the teacher
- school should be an exciting environment for the child
- the curriculum should be child-centred
- the teacher acts in the role of facilitator
- basic skills are important but should be balanced with life-skills
- experiential learning is central
- artistic stimulus should be provided
- school should be democratically run as a preparation for life
- there should be links to the community
- school should meet all the needs of the child, physical, emotional and intellectual

(adapted from Koetzsch 1997: 9–10)

One of the central ideas within Dewey's philosophy was the concept of 'reconciling dualisms' (Fishman 1998: 15). Most Western philosophies focus on the separation of such aspects as the 'self' and 'the world', but according to Dewey, such a division is too simplistic, as opposing forces are interdependent and interact. He considered that the most important dualities were:

- the individual versus the group
- creativity versus appreciation
- the impulse versus reflection
- the student versus the curriculum

Dewey approached learning through a series of questions to deal with problems (Fishman 1998: 17):

- What are the dichotomous activities within our dilemmas?
- How might they be better integrated and balanced?

He also valued greatly the idea that learning goes far beyond the school setting. 'Learning in its broadest, non-school sense, is a reconciliation of tensions between the self and its surroundings' (Fishman 1998: 19). The features of such non-school learning, Dewey felt, could be harnessed to make school more interesting. He believed that the learning process encompasses emotions and feelings as well as cognitive aspects. Central to Dewey's philosophy was the quality of the student experience. His concept of 'continuity' relates to the fact that experiences are complex in terms of time; current experience is rooted in the past and has its outcomes in the future. By 'interaction' Dewey means that experiences are complex spatially, too, and involve interaction between the organism and its environment. This may include books, experiments or subject content, for example. According to Dewey, these are 'the longitudinal and lateral aspects of experience' (Dewey 1938: 44 in Fishman 1998: 30).

Despite his move away from formal religion, his interpretation is strangely reflective of Buddhist concepts, which would make his theories very attractive to an educationalist like Tsunesaburo Makiguchi, who was developing similar ideas across the other side of the world. Dewey wanted schools to help students become empowered, to discover their vocation, to explore cultural values and find freedom through cooperative learning. For him, 'enriched experience' has meaning that is not fixed but builds towards 'an emotionally satisfying end' (Fishman 1998: 31). However, not all experiences are educative; this depends on the quality of the interactions that have to lead to an outcome, for example, completing a piece of writing. Students are constantly reconstructing themselves and their own meaning through the interactions of the classroom – pupil to pupil, teacher to pupil and pupil to environment. Dewey's approach to teaching focuses on the positive, that is, encouraging students to write well rather than focusing on correcting grammar.

One of the key dualities according to Dewey (Fishman 1998) is that of construction or impulses versus criticism. They are opposites but also interdependent, as impulse without some form of criticality becomes 'a mere gush' (Dewey 1938: 139 in Fishman 1998: 35), while criticism needs to lead to further creation, otherwise learning remains sterile. In the duality of student versus curriculum, students' interests should be harnessed in order for them to engage fully in learning, but students should not be allowed to be too self-indulgent, as in 'progressive education'. Students need to be challenged in order to deepen their thinking and their interest. Effort is also required, but this should be voluntary, not stemming from fear of punishment.

For students to engage fully in learning interactions, they need goals that are meaningful to them, they need to focus on the means for achieving those goals, for example course materials. They should also be enabled to work from the familiar to the unfamiliar, using knowledge and experiences from the past as bridges to understand new experience. The curriculum, therefore, must be stimulating and challenging but not beyond the students' capabilities. Dewey also favoured project learning, provided the subject matter was worthwhile.

For Dewey, education was not just about the individual, it had a responsibility to develop moral and cooperative human beings. Central to this is the concept of taking responsibility, that is, taking ownership of the learning. Personal and social growth come together, personal happiness through education should not be at the expense of the happiness of others. All these ideas are remarkably current in education today and are testimony to the enduring nature of Dewey's work.

During his lifetime, Dewey's influence was able to spread through his work at Columbia's Teachers' College, and was important in shaping the primary curriculum in the USA in particular. During World War 2, progressive education fell out of favour as nations demanded a more instrumental role for education. However, following the publication of A. S. Neill's book *Summerhill* in the 1960s, humanist/progressive ideas became popular once more.

Dewey's legacy includes such practices as cooperative learning, multicultural education, the social curriculum, conflict-solving, developmental education and even open-plan classrooms. During the 1980s, however, governments in countries such as the United States and the United Kingdom became anxious about the economic downturn, which led to a backlash in educational policy and to an emphasis on standardized curricula and the centrality of assessment. Progressive practices have, however, continued to flourish in alternative schools.

---

### Activity 7.4

- What have been your experiences of cooperative learning?
- Can you think of other examples from your own school experience that reflect ideas put forward by Dewey?

---

# Makiguchi (1871–1944)

Soka Education was a system developed by a Japanese primary headteacher, Tsunesaburo Makiguchi, in early twentieth century Japan, and through the efforts of two of his followers, Josei Toda and Daisaku Ikeda, this system is now flourishing in a number of countries.

In 1913, at the age of 42, Makiguchi was appointed as principal of a primary school in Tokyo and he worked as a headteacher for some 20 years. He was aware of the writings of John Dewey in the United States and was already formulating proposals for the reform of the education system in Japan along philosophical lines similar to Dewey's. For example, both men wanted to put the child at the centre of both theory and practice, which was far removed from what was happening in Japan at the time. According to Makiguchi, the main purpose of education was the happiness of the child, a philosophy that was revolutionary in early twentieth century Japan.

> I am driven by the intense desire to prevent the present deplorable situation – ten million of our children and students forced to endure the agonies of cutthroat competition, the difficulty of getting into good schools, the 'examination hell' and the struggle for jobs after graduation – from afflicting the next generation. (Makiguchi 1930 in Ikeda 2001: 9)

At the time of his writing, the Japanese education system was focused on abstract theory while experiential learning was totally disregarded. However, Makiguchi stressed the centrality of experience in the learning process, including encouraging teachers to reflect on their day-to-day teaching, out of which reflection theory would develop. This, of course, is not too far removed from some aspects of professional practice in the UK (although practitioners are not allowed the freedom of devising their own theory).

Having become a headteacher in a very poor area of Tokyo in 1920, Makiguchi determined to treat all pupils equally, refusing to favour the children of the rich, as was customary at the time. He even proposed the abolition of local government inspections and direct intervention in the day-to-day organization of schools. What he advocated was a democratic education system with participation by teachers and parents, and he saw education as a process of learning to learn, completely in contrast to the transmission model of teaching that is still favoured in modern-day Japan. Teachers were, in fact, facilitators, and children, autonomous learners who were seeking to create value in the world, with teachers 'guiding' their progress. Teachers, themselves, were encouraged to remain active learners and engage in personal development.

Makiguchi took the notion of truth, goodness and beauty, popular in Japan at the time, and substituted the concept of benefit for that of truth:

> He defined beauty as that which brings fulfilment to the aesthetic sensibility of the individual; benefit as that which advances the life of the individual in a holistic manner; goodness as that which contributes to the well-being of the larger human society. (Ikeda 2001: 16)

By value, he means here something that can affect the human condition, either positively or negatively but that is not fixed – that is, values can change depending on the perspective. In 1930, Makiguchi established the organization Soka Gakkai, translating as 'value-creating society', and proceeded to put into practice his belief that education should be linked to daily life and be part of the experience of living, not something removed or compartmentalized. According to Makiguchi there were six necessary transformational processes, the details of which are highlighted in Figure 7.1 (see Ikeda 2001: 20).

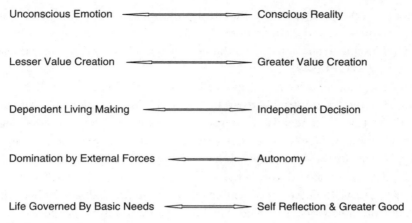

**Figure 7.1.** The Transformational Process.
*Source:* Based on Ikeda (2001: 20).

Due to his refusal to be bound by the imposition of totalitarian laws, during World War 2, Makiguchi was attacked as a 'thought criminal' for his adherence to Dewey's principles that democratic ends need democratic methods and, further, that reverting to 'absolutist procedures is a betrayal of human freedom' (Dewey 1939: 13 in Ikeda 2001: 21).

In July 1943, Makiguchi and his mentee, Josei Toda, were arrested by the Special Higher Police and imprisoned. He was 72 at the time and spent the next 500 days in solitary confinement, still refusing to recant and accept that the emperor was a divine being and that Japan was engaged in a holy war. Sadly, he died in prison on 18 November 1944.

Although Dewey had moved away from organized religion, both he and Makiguchi shared the belief that the purpose of religion is to serve human beings, not the other way round. The values of reality, people and experience that Makiguchi held as central to the purpose of education were also the core of Dewey's philosophy. However, through a process of empirical research, Makiguchi came eventually to the Buddhism of a thirteenth century Japanese priest, Nichiren Daishonin, which he saw as reflecting and supporting his educational theory of value.

> Life is the most precious of all treasures. Even the treasures of the entire universe cannot equal the value of a single human life. (Nichiren Daishonin)

Today, through the work of Makiguchi's devoted followers, Soka schools exist in many countries (Brazil, Hong Kong, Malaysia, Singapore and South Korea). They have been established on the basis that 'all children should be afforded the opportunity to develop their potential limitlessly and to lead fulfilling lives undeterred by the destructive influences of society' (Ikeda 2001: 37). Soka schools belong to a private system and provide education from early years through to university level. The focus of the organization is 'value-creation' in society, and although inspired by Buddhist philosophy, they do not teach a particular religious doctrine within the curriculum. The schools see their mission as being able to 'foster a rich humanism and spirituality that will enable students to enjoy personal growth and freedom' (Ikeda 2001: 49).

Makiguchi's vision of education has become a reality through the determination of Daisaku Ikeda, who has continued to argue that to make education subordinate to both bureaucratic and political agendas is a grave error, as is also the vain hope that a strict national curriculum will 'solve' the enormous economic problems faced by many countries today. He puts forward the proposal that the conventional paradigm should be turned on its head, that is, we should not consider what education can do for society but rather how society can serve the needs of education. He refers to the dialogue he had with Robert Thurman of Columbia University, who stated that 'education is the purpose of human life' (Ikeda 2001: 70).

*Soka Education* is based on the idea that education should help people turn negative human attributes, for example conflict and dislike, into positive attributes. This will be achieved through developing an understanding of the link between individuals and the community, and through dialogue and transcending differences. Following on from the first G8 summit on Education in April 2000, Ikeda presented a vision of a 'United Nations of Education' where education would be freed from the interference of politics. International understanding and dialogue, made possible through a system of educational exchange, would help to create global peace.

Ikeda also recommended volunteering with tangible outcomes as one way for young people to engage with society and the environment, and he advocates the empowerment of teachers to free them from the imposition of national reforms. The ideal Soka curriculum includes the following:

- peace education
- environmental education
- development education, including issues of poverty and global justice
- human rights education to awaken an awareness of human equality and dignity

There are currently two Soka universities, one on the outskirts of Tokyo and one in Aliso Viejo, California. The core curriculum in the latter consists of major questions:

- What is an individual human life?
- What is the relationship between the individual and the physical environment in which we live?
- What is the relationship between the individual and the human environment?
- What are the global issues in peace, culture and education?

Soka Universities actively pursue international exchanges as a way of fostering greater cross-cultural understanding, and English is regarded as the language that will facilitate such a globalized education system. Closely linked to this idea is the importance of global citizenship, which develops:

- the wisdom to perceive the interconnectedness of all things
- the courage not to fear or deny difference but to respect and strive to understand people of different cultures
- the compassion to have empathy for people across the world

These aims are reminiscent of Dewey's work, where the local community is presented as the place where the spirit of global citizenship is generated.

---

## My Soka Education

### *By Yukiko Davenne*

I entered Kansai Soka Junior High School and Senior High School, where my life was changed, when I was 12 years old.

I was so shy, I had never been true to myself and wanted to change that life to the one in which I could live true to myself and just as I was. The surroundings of the school were beautiful, with lots of the beauty of nature in a rural setting, which was completely different from a big city where I lived. I could not wait to go to school every morning even though it took me nearly two hours each way.

I met so many wonderful people there. I was impressed, especially by the rules made by students not by teachers. For instance, a rule of greeting people, where you said, 'Hello, good morning, how are you?' and so on to every person you met on the way to school from the nearest railway station, which was 20 minutes' walking distance. In Japan, we normally do not greet each other unless you know each other. What was great was that all of these rules were made by students, who had a passion to make our school something we can be proud of, and did it joyfully.

Another thing I found totally different from my previous experience in school, was that we were always encouraged to make poems and songs. Before, I hardly paid attention to nature. I had to look to the beauty of nature in order to create poems, which was not difficult to my surprise. Finding the beauty of nature and having a sense of wonder became my greatest habit or something I always find and feel without even trying.

The most amazing thing of all was that we had a great founder, called Mr Daisaku Ikeda, who is the president of Soka Gakkai International (SGI), an international Buddhist organization. He used to come to school quite often, although he was such a busy person, as you can imagine from the fact that he has never had even a single day off since he joined SGI 61 years ago, apart from the short period he spent in hospital. He has had thousands of dialogues with the world leaders of peace, scholars and so on. We had some of his friends as guests at our school and I was privileged to welcome them with the Japanese old tradition of the tea ceremony, just because I was one of the members of tea ceremony club.

I was stimulated to open up my way of thinking by meeting different people from all over the world, and my curiosity, wanting to know more about the world, was getting bigger and bigger. That was the time for me to have a dream of living in the UK and working for world peace. That time was the late '70s and early '80s, we rarely saw any foreign people even in Osaka, which is the second biggest city, after Tokyo, in Japan.

Mr Ikeda sent the students all sorts of presents, along with messages and poems every time he travelled inside Japan and abroad. He played sports with us, studied with us in our classrooms, gazed at stars together, chatted, rang the families whose children stayed in dormitories at the school

> ### My Soka Education—cont'd
>
> because they live so far away. We felt his care, love, compassion and prayers for us to be happy and be great leaders, who work hard for people's happiness and world peace just as he has been. He showed us how to live with the profound mission by his actions, which is completely opposite of the lives with shallow desires and emptiness. He is an action man.
>
> My year was only the fifth year since the school opened. The teachers were young, too. They also had an enthusiastic attitude for their way of teaching and dealing with the pupils. Some teachers used the outside rather than classrooms to teach us. They were sincere to teach and help our lives. Of course, we were just teenagers, sometimes we did not like some of the teachers and tried to be a bit rebellious. However, somehow we managed to sort everything out by ourselves.
>
> We have had regular meetings for all of our Soka School graduates after graduating. We care for each other and we do not see any of the surfaces of our lives, such as jobs, houses, status and life styles. We are just what we were at school. We share our struggles and joys, even though I live thousands of miles away. I see them every time I go back to Japan.
>
> Finally, I cannot express enough my gratitude to my parents who sent met to this greatest school, despite the great financial struggle it caused them. I repay my gratitude all my life.
>
> Thank you.
>
> Yukiko Davenne

# A. S. Neill (1883–1973)

In 1921, A. S. Neill founded what is possibly the most famous alternative school ever, Summerhill. The school is unique and is regarded as 'the oldest children's democracy in the world' (Vaughan 2006: Preface). During the 1960s and 1970s, a number of radically different schools were founded, but few survived and not without having to compromise on their initial aims and methods, unlike Summerhill, which has remained true to its original aims.

Neill was a teacher who had spent a long time working in state schools, which he regarded as producing 'uncreative citizens who want docile, uncreative children who will fit into a civilisation whose standard of success is money' (Neill 1968 in Vaughan 2006: 6). He rejected the principles on which most schools were based and committed himself to an approach that took as its starting point the belief that children are inherently 'good'. His original idea was to create a school that would fit the children rather than the other way round; he believed that children should be left alone to develop naturally, with the end result that they would become confident and happy members of society.

## The aims of Summerhill

The aims of Summerhill (see website) are:

- to allow children freedom to grow emotionally
- to give children power over their own lives

- to give children time to develop naturally
- to create a happier childhood by removing fear and coercion from their lives

Lessons are optional at Summerhill, although they are timetabled and, according to Neill (in Vaughan 2006), most children would attend eventually, although the school remained true to its original principles of never forcing a child to attend anything.

> The function of the child is to live his (sic) own life – not the life that his anxious parents think he should live, nor a life according to the purpose of the educator who thinks he knows what is best.
> (Neill 1968 in Vaughan 2006: 12)

Neill shared the view of other philosophers we have considered in this chapter that the aim of life is to become happy and that education is central to that process; it should be a 'preparation for life' (Vaughan 2006: 21).

## The structure of the school

Summerhill was opened as a small residential school catering for both boys and girls. Numbers of pupils ranged from 45 to 80 with many coming from such places as Australia, Japan and Scandinavia. It was divided into three age groups: 5–7, 8–10 and 11–15, although some pupils stayed on to take college entrance examinations. Neill admitted, and subsequent inspections of the school supported his view, that teaching methods were not particularly radical, largely because Neill did not consider teaching itself to be of particular importance.

The curriculum offered did cover the expected subject range such as Science, Maths and languages, but Neill maintained that the majority of the standard school curriculum was irrelevant to children. He firmly believed that learning came second to play and that learning should not be disguised as play in order to make it more acceptable. In this, he went a stage further than most of the educational thinkers we have been discussing. Nor did he have a lot of respect for the competitive regime of examinations, although Summerhill students who wished to were encouraged and supported in their applications.

Subject lessons were supplemented with 'private lessons' with pupils with particular issues or problems, and these were a form of therapy sessions, which Neill claimed 'were really a re-education. Their object was to lop off all the complexes resulting from morality and fear' (Neill 1968 in Vaughan 2006: 33). Neill regarded practical civics as being one of the most important aspects of the educational experience the pupils received and, as such, established the school 'as a self-governing school, democratic in form' (Vaughan 2006: 41).

All school rules and decisions were decided during the weekly General Meeting at which teachers and pupils alike held an equal vote. Neill noted that the most exciting topics that came up were always connected with food. Through this process of voicing opinions, students were encouraged in public speaking resulting in increased self-confidence. Neill believed that if children were free to develop their self-esteem then there would be little need for them to engage in anti-social behaviour, indeed commenting that teachers rarely lost their tempers.

For Neill, the community of the school was paramount yet he did not believe that his role was to reform society but to bring happiness to a small number of children. This, of course, is a more modest ambition than other radical educationalists, Dewey and Makiguchi, for example. Furthermore, Neill declared that all children will succeed in life if left alone, success being defined as 'the ability to work joyfully and live positively' (Vaughan 2006: 24). According to this definition, most of Summerhill's pupils have become successful in life, some in a range of professions, even though, by Neill's own admission, some also left without the basic skills of reading and writing.

## Summerhill and the Inspectors

In 1949, Her Majesty's Inspectors visited the school and among the comments in their report was a note that there was an 'absence of any kind of religious life or instruction' (Neill 1968: 55), the effects of which they felt unable to judge in the course of their short visit. They also observed that some teaching methods were surprisingly formal and outdated. Their overall conclusions, however, were that the children were:

> . . . full of life and zest. Of boredom and apathy there was no sign . . . their lack of shyness and self-consciousness made them very easy, pleasant people to get on with. (Ibid.: 59)

All of these opinions reflect the aims that Neill had expounded from the beginning.

In 1999, a further inspection, this time by Ofsted, produced a very different report. Complaints included the statement that both the curriculum and education provided at the school were 'fragmented, disjointed and likely to adversely affect their future options' (HMI 1999 in Stronach 2006: 120). The list of requirements was such that the school would inevitably have to close. In 2000, the school successfully appealed against these complaints and consequently the school remains open to this day. The barrister arguing on behalf of the school in the tribunal in 2000, commented that Neill's educational legacy was still alive and that:

> . . . the system he devised to nurture humanity in children so that they could fulfil their real potential in life works as well as it ever did. (Geoffrey Robertson Q. C. in Stronach 2006: 125)

---

### Activity 7.5

Look back to the aims of Summerhill at the beginning of this section and evaluate them according to your own view of the purposes of education. What do you think are the lessons we can learn from the Summerhill experience with regard to state education?

# Summary

In this chapter we have looked at the work of educational philosophers whose ideas have had a considerable influence on the ideologies that inform the organization and curriculum of schools in the UK and elsewhere. The ones we have studied have generally been in the tradition broadly known as progressive or Romantic. They all share the belief that education should be child-centred and that human beings are essentially noble creatures. They do not always agree fully with each other. Neill, for example, believed that Montessori's methods were artificial and completely lacked creativity (Neill in Vaughan 2006: 21). Some have argued that the purpose of education is to establish a more harmonious society, while others have focused wholly on the needs of the individual. They have all tried to present an alternative to the state and independent systems that, according to Geoffrey Robertson Q. C., in his defence of Summerhill in 2000, 'have not found ways of combating racism, bullying, sexual abuse, and which are strait-jacketed by a narrow National Curriculum and undermined by large classes, and where the tyranny of examination results is worse than ever' (transcript from Tribunal 2000 in Stronach, 2006: 125).

As we shall see, there are those who would disagree with the views expressed in this chapter. However, their legacy overall can be seen in education systems today in terms of the respect for children's views that you would find written into most schools' policies.

## Recommended reading

Apple, M. W. (2004), *Ideology and Curriculum* (third edition). New York & London: Routledge Falmer.

Noddings, N. (2007), *Philosophy of Education*. Colorado: Westview Press.

## Useful websites

www.summerhillschool.co.uk
  The website of A. S. Neill's Summerhill School
www.infed.org/thinkers/index.htm
  The online encyclopaedia of informal education provides information on educational thinkers
www.sokaeducation.org
  The website for Soka schools and universities

# Part Four
## The Contexts of Education

# Formal Contexts for Learning 8

## The learning society and notions of formal, informal and non-formal education

### The learning society

A discussion of the 'learning society' might seem a strange place to start an exploration of the diversity of *formal* contexts in which education takes place, however, it is the discussions around the notion of 'lifelong learning' and the 'learning society' that have been used to frame the definitions of formal, informal and non-formal learning. The debates have raged for many years around the distinctions between the various 'types' of learning and their roles within the continuum of educational and learning opportunities available to an individual throughout their life. Although we allude to those distinctions in this section of the book, we draw you away from discussions around the *kind* of learning that is taking place, to focus rather on the *contexts* themselves, and the diversity of 'learning places' that constitute an educational system.

In 1972, UNESCO produced the 'Faure Report: Learning to Be', which introduced the notion of a 'learning society' and the concept of *lifelong education* (Morgan-Klein and

Osborne 2007). The report suggested that *lifelong learning* would be one of the major forces shaping educational systems in the future. As a concept, lifelong learning encapsulates notions of both formal and non-formal education, and is concerned with issues of social justice and access to education for all (Morgan-Klein and Osborne 2008). Later, in 1995, the European Union in their White Paper, 'Towards the Learning Society' formulated lifelong learning as a *strategy* in response to the perceived emerging consequences of globalization and new technologies. Although not a new concept, *learning through life*, which was once associated mainly with adult vocational training, has now become embedded within educational doctrine and policy, and, with varying emphases, within educational systems across Europe (ibid.).

There are a number of critics of the concept of lifelong learning who suggest that it is too focused on vocational training and employability rather than on the more social aspects of learning. An alternative concept to lifelong learning, with a similar focus on employability, is the OECDs model of 'recurrent education', which envisages individuals revisiting education at various times in order to develop their careers.

## Formal, informal and non-formal education

What has arisen from the consideration of notions of the learning society, is a definition of three types of '*learning systems*':

> **Formal education** or learning is usually institutionalized in schools and colleges etc. It is highly structured, based on different stages, has externally determined outcomes and leads to certification.
> **Informal education** is a lifelong process in which individuals learn from their environment – from the variety of everyday experiences, from their family, friends, work and the media.
> **Non-formal education** or learning is not institutionalized, nor does it lead to formal certification. It falls outside of traditional formal education. However, it is structured and intentional.

Many people do not agree with such distinctions, suggesting that they simply exist to make categorization and association easy, so that, for example, formal education is associated with schools, non-formal education with community groups and other organizations and informal with all the 'other' situations. Others view learning as something that takes place all the time, whatever individuals are engaged in, and suggest that most learning, therefore, takes place outside of what we would term formal educational activities (Billet 2001 in Colley et al. 2002). The debates around conceptions of formal, informal and non-formal education have resonance with those surrounding notions of education and schooling, and according to Hull and Greeno (2007) rely on two commonly held assumptions or possible misconceptions:

1. that the ways in which people learn and develop differ depending on the context
2. that informal learning is always supplemental to what is learnt in a formal context such as school

As Bekerman et al. suggest, it may therefore be better to consider that:

> . . . *learning* (is) something that happens in a variety of places and to think of these places as sites that generate learning in a variety of forms, which should force us to reconsider the meaning of 'a good education'. (Bekerman et al. 2006: 2)

This notion, that learning occurs in a variety of forms, to a large extent dependent upon the context or place in which that learning is situated, is one that we will be adopting in our following discussions. In this chapter and in the following chapters in this section of the book, we will, therefore, be exploring the diversity of contexts in which education and learning can take place. First we will consider the formal contexts that provide an alternative to mainstream state schooling, which we outlined in Chapter 5, while in the following chapters we will explore a variety of other 'learning places', such as museums and theatres and also a range of 'alternative education' contexts that serve the needs of children who are either excluded from, or unable to participate in, normal schooling.

# Choice – and the diversity of provision

There has always been a diversity of provision of 'formal' schooling in England, in which the Church and other voluntary organizations have played a small but significant part. However, most people had little say in the type of formal schooling their children received. According to Edwards, 'until the 1980s, choice of school was largely confined to families able to pay school fees, or buy a house in an educationally favourable area, or (who) had the confidence to reject a bureaucratically allocated place and press for something else' (Edwards 2002: 114).

Since then, consecutive governments have sought to please the parents among their electorate with promises of greater choice and more diversity of provision within the state system. There is no space in this debate to detail the changes and reforms to the structure of formal schooling that have since taken place. Suffice to say that in the intervening period there has been the near demise of both the grammar school and the 'bog standard' comprehensive. What remains in their place is a complex picture of growing independent and faith-based sectors alongside a diversified traditional state schooling comprising local education authority run community schools, Foundation and Trust schools, voluntary aided or controlled schools (including faith-based schools), specialist schools, academies, city technology colleges, community and foundation special schools, grammar schools and maintained boarding schools.

The flagship of these changes, according to the government, is the academy, which is basically a state funded, independent school. Such schools, while receiving funding from the state, also receive a £2 million grant from a sponsor who can be either from the voluntary sector, business or a faith-based organization. As a result, such schools have more independence and flexibility than traditional state schools (Driver and Martell 2006). As a consequence, both the nature of the 'privatization' of state education and the nature and role of the sponsors has come in for considerable criticism.

> . . . the Labour leadership has come to see independent schools as providing a template of potential solutions to the intractable problems of state schools. It is not too far from the truth to say that current government education policy is to make state schools as much like independent schools as possible. (Morrison 2007: 3)

---

### Activity 8.1

What do you think the role of the state should be in providing formal education?

Do you think that there should be more privately funded schools or simply more private funding going into state schools like academies?

Would you be in favour of a voucher system so that parents could really choose what kind of education they wanted for their children?

Are there any problems that you can envisage if we continue with a programme of choice and diversification?

---

# Independent schools

*The 'public school' narrative poses particular problems . . . In this narrative 'public school' is a term of mild abuse . . . (it) is (a narrative) of unearned and self-perpetuating privilege. It is embodied in the character created by the comedian Harry Enfield and known as Tim Nice-but-Dim: a white male of limited intelligence but large bank-balance whose public school accent and networks give him undeserved access to elite positions denied to more talented individuals educated in the state sector.*

*(Morrison 2007: 3)*

There has always been a small but important independent sector in the UK. It currently educates around 671,000 children in around 2,600 independent schools, representing around 7 per cent of the total number of schoolchildren in the UK. The majority of these pupils are day pupils, and only a small proportion boarders. There are slightly more boys than girls in private schools, with the majority of pupils being of secondary age. A growing number of pupils are from overseas (mainly Hong Kong, China and Europe), and a number are the children of parents who work abroad (ISC Census 2008).

The private, or as it has become known, the independent sector, has always been a 'main source of overtly selective secondary schooling' (Edwards 2002: 111). According to Adonis and Pollard, private schooling has become:

> . . . the natural choice of a 'super-class' of 'higher' professionals and managers, thereby producing a 'two nations' school system in which the children's location is even more socially determined than in the past. (Adonis and Pollard 1998 in Edwards 2002: 111)

## Why pay?

Private education (or confusingly, public schooling) has always been the domain of the rich and powerful. However, a large number of parents on more modest incomes are willing to pay for their child's education. Although the original reason for many parents choosing to educate privately, i.e. failure to gain a place at a 'grammar school' within the then selective state system, has disappeared, many parents still opt against sending their children to their local state school. There are a number of reasons why people are willing to pay for an education, including:

- social and academic privilege
- greater resources
- greater choice in the type of education provided
- the ethos of the school
- the type of peer group
- smaller pupil/teacher ratios (9.6 to 1)

## The benefits

One of the key issues relating to independent education is whether it is actually superior to state education. The statistics would suggest that an investment in private education does produce tangible benefits for students. For example, in terms of GCSE results, 28.5 per cent of pupils in independent schools gained A* grades (national average: 6.8 per cent) and 59.2 per cent of all exam entries were graded A* or A compared to a national average of 20.7 per cent. There are similar differentials between the performance of independent school pupils at A level and those in state schools (ISC Census 2008). However, one of the most telling statistics is that despite the fact that less than 10 per cent of pupils attend independent schools, nearly 50 per cent of them enter Oxford or Cambridge, and the majority of elite positions in this country are still dominated by the alumni from a few top private schools (Sullivan and Heath 2002). However, it should be remembered that there are schools that do not have such a record of success.

Research into the differentials in outcomes between private and state schools remains unclear as to the reasons. In the main they are those we listed above, i.e. parents are selecting those schools for the very reasons those schools are so effective, although determining the contribution of individual factors such as parental background, resourcing and pupil/teacher ratios to that success is complex (Sullivan and Heath 2002).

The debate about the role of the independent sector in providing alternative formal educational provision will continue. The advocates of private schooling suggest that private schools are more effective and better run than state schools and are capable of responding to the demands of parents. They are also well placed to survive in the highly competitive, market-based education system in the UK. The opponents of private education, on the other hand, present a duality of arguments, pointing to the fact that in one way private schools unfairly advantage certain groups within society, and in another way, their success is largely determined by the ability and affluence of their intake (Sullivan and Heath 2008).

---

**Activity 8.2**

- How divisive a force do you think private education is within society?
- Do you think we should be promoting the privatization of our state schools?
- Do you think that big business has a role to play in providing education?

---

# Faith schools

Since medieval times, faith organizations have been involved in educational provision in Europe, generally offering schooling for many disadvantaged children before mass state education came into being. In England, it was the Church of England that first played a major role in educational provision for the poor:

> Between 1811 and 1860, the Church of England founded 17,000 schools through its National Society to offer education to the poor . . . The first Jewish school for the poor was set up in 1732 and from 1852 the Catholic Bishops have worked to make available, wherever possible, schools for all Catholic children regardless of their parents' ability to pay. (DFCSF 2007: 2)

Church provision of schooling, however, was patchy and in 1870, the government stepped in to fill in the gaps with the provision of state-funded schools for the working classes. At the end of the nineteenth century there was an expansion in the numbers of Catholic schools and also the provision of schools by Methodists and Quakers. Following the Education Act of 1902, most faith schools were taken over by local education authorities, as the state now guaranteed compulsory Christian education. Since the 1944 Education Act, faith and non-faith schools have existed side by side in local authorities.

> Arrangements to include faith-based schools within the scope of public funding are the product of centuries of wrangling and compromise, and are not based on universal and perennial principles grounded in commitments to pluralism or to religious freedom. The argument should now be

conducted – once again, with an appreciation of its history . . . in terms of values and principles adapted to contemporary British Society and its needs. The novel circumstances of this century require a new framework for political discourse: new bottles for new wine. (Judge 2002: 427)

Currently, parents who want their children to have a faith-based education are able to do so, provided that there is a suitable state school in their locality. At present, about one third of all schools in the maintained sector in England are schools with a 'religious character', the vast majority of which are Christian (DCSF 2007). Since 1997, other denominations have come under the umbrella of maintained schools: Muslim, Sikh, Seventh Day Adventist and Greek Orthodox. The first Hindu primary school opened in September 2008. Significantly, almost a third of the new academies have a faith designation and a religious sponsor. Similarly, around 40 per cent of the independent schools we referred to earlier are described as having a religious character. Some religious groups are now collaborating to open 'multi-faith schools', for example there is a current initiative for such a school between the Church of England and a Muslim organization in Oldham, which may offer a more balanced approach to teaching about religion (Marley 2007).

Since Labour came to power in 1997, most applications to open new faith schools have been accepted, while many of the new academies are being sponsored by religious organizations as indicated above (TES 2006). It has also been made clear, following the launch of the document 'Faith in the System' (2007), that the rise in the number of religious schools is set to continue with full government support. Moreover, there will be help in the form of funding for those schools that are planning to move from private status into the state sector and that do not have the means of improving facilities.

The vision, which is shared by both government and the providers of publicly funded schools with a religious character, emphasizes the 'very positive contribution' made by faith schools in their respective communities. The role of faith-based schools is seen as:

- helping to meet the needs of those 'who would otherwise be hard to reach'
- providing education 'for the wider society' while 'promoting community cohesion'
- satisfying the wishes of parents
- helping to drive up standards

(DCSF 2007)

The 'Faith in the System' proposals also increase the powers of faith-based schools in order to allow religious background to be taken into consideration when appointing or promoting support staff as well as teaching staff, and to ensure that all aspects of the school life are in keeping with the relevant religious belief (DCSF 2007). However, the most controversial area is that relating to admissions, following an embarrassing change in government policy forced on Alan Johnson, the then Secretary of State for Education. He had been pressing for new faith schools to offer guaranteed places to children of a different or no faith, but had backed down in the face of opposition from religious leaders (Stewart 2007). Instead, the 'Faith in the System' document sets out that schools can give priority for 'some or all of their places to children from the faith concerned when they are oversubscribed' (DCSF 2007: 16), but does make special reference to children in care.

## Issues

There are a number of issues and debates that surround the provision of schools 'with a religious character' within the state funded school system:

- Should governments encourage and fund faith-based schooling?
- Does faith-based education lead to segregation?
- What kinds of benefits accrue from faith-based education?

### *The benefits*

There is contradictory research as to whether faith schools provide better general education for their pupils than schools with no religious affiliation. Sander and Krautmann, writing about Catholic schools in the United States, refer to a number of studies that have indicated that Catholic schools have a positive effect on academic achievement (Bryk et al. 1993 and Chubb and Moe 1990 in Sander and Krautmann 1995: 217), although there is an acknowledgement that results could be affected by the fact that most of these schools are selective in their intake. In their own study, they conclude that second year students in Catholic high schools are more likely to graduate with their peers, but are no more likely to stay on in education beyond high school. They also point out that Catholic schools, which dominate the private sector in the United States, admit fewer pupils with disabilities and are positively affected by their location within the social capital of their Catholic community (ibid.). Recent research in England by Allen and West (2007) reveals that religious secondary schools do not serve the most disadvantaged and generally have a more affluent intake and fewer pupils on free school meals (Marley 2007).

> The superior performance attributed to . . . church schools . . . because they are what they are diminishes into insignificance when intake composition is taken into account. (Edwards 2002: 117)

### *Should the state pay?*

If faith-based schools do not provide a better education, what other reasons could there be for the state continuing to fund them? According to Judge, the state funding of faith-based schools is based on the following assumptions:

- religion has an important part to play in the education of every child
- the rights of the families to provide religious education for their children are not to be challenged
- confessional schools supported by state funding have played an important part in British education
- confessional schools are often effective

(Judge 2002: 427)

However, as Judge remarks, although these present a reasonable premise on which to base an argument for the state funding of faith-based schools, 'does it therefore follow that there should be *more* faith-based schooling? (2002: 428)

---

### Activity 8.3

At a time when the influence of organized religion appears to be declining, do you think that it is reasonable to fund more faith-based education?
  Do you think there should be:

- No faith-based education?
- Segregation of faith-based education into the private sector?
- The kind of 'flexible accommodation' we have today? (see Judge 2002)

Can you think of any negative consequences of the state providing the funding of 'education of a religious character', particularly that of minority faiths within society?

---

### *Are we 'sleepwalking our way to segregation'?*

Teachers' leaders have argued that faith schools are essentially divisive rather than encouraging equality and diversity, and that their admissions policies do nothing to promote community cohesion. This echoes the warning from Sir Trevor Phillips (Haythrop Institute 2005), the then Chair of the Commission for Racial Equality, quoted above, that children are being segregated more in such schools than they are in their communities, leading to younger generations becoming less well integrated than their parents.

Religious leaders have countered these arguments by suggesting that there is no evidence that faith schools contribute to religious conflict, pointing to the fact that many secular schools have problems with divisions among pupils (Heythrop Institute 2005). They also assert that faith schools can provide a coherent framework of understanding for the appreciation of difference and that children can be helped to become 'religiously literate' (TES 2008). One other important issue remains, that of parental freedom of choice. Which leads us to the question that if faith schools were to be closed, which denominations, if any, would be allowed to remain? Does England still regard itself as a largely Christian society, when no more than 4 per cent of the parents of children attending faith schools attend church? (The Secular Society in Stewart 2006).

## Home education

As we have seen in Chapter 7, there have always been radical educationalists who have presented alternative ways of organizing schools and the curriculum, each with their own preferred aims and purposes. However, most have continued to operate within systems that we would all recognize as schools. There has also been what Apple (2007: 2) calls a 'social movement' of teaching children in the home itself, which, historically, was the prerogative of the aristocracy and upper middle classes (Meighan 1997), but since the 1970s has enjoyed a renewal of interest in the USA and the UK (Koetzsch 1997; Meighan 1997).

According to Apple (2007), homeschooling challenges one of the key assumptions in society, which is that teaching is carried out by people who are 'teachers' and that it takes place in institutions called 'schools'. Apple (2001) also presents a powerful argument that warns us that we should be wary of this challenge, stating that unless state schooling reinvents itself dramatically in order to meet the needs of learners in the twenty-first century, the principles of homeschooling could pose a real threat to the cohesion of society.

## Historical perspectives

*School is a twelve year jail sentence where bad habits are the only curriculum truly learned. I teach school and win awards doing it. I should know.*

*(Gatto 1992 in Meighan 1997: 49)*

According to Meighan (1997), 'Education Otherwise' began life as a small cooperative following a meeting of like-minded people in Swindon in 1977. It was acknowledged that many children had been homeschooled in the past, such as the violinist Yehudi Menhuin, but the phenomenon was relatively new for 'ordinary' people. Since then, the movement has grown and there are now about 20,000 homeschooled children in the UK (Meighan 2007) and the figure is steadily growing.

The tradition of criticizing state schooling has become more widespread since the 1970s, and withdrawing completely from a system, perceived to be inadequate from many perspectives, is the logical final step for some parents. After all, as Meighan reminds us, schools were established in what he terms 'information poor environments' (1997: 4). Now, thanks to the internet and technological advances, this is no longer true.

Today we need flexible, adaptable people and the production-line approach (of schools) is not noted for this. (Meighan 1997: 4)

Apple (2001) also traces the growth in popularity of homeschooling in the USA back to the economic downturn in the 1970s and the belief that the state was stifling personal freedom and denying choice to the 'consumer'. Worse still, liberal bureaucrats and welfare systems were perceived to be attacking 'family values' and taking over the role of the parent. Stories about poor teachers contributed to the popular myths about teaching being a career that indulged self-seeking individuals only attracted to the profession because of the generous working conditions. Apple (2001) also cites groups such as the Christian Women of America, who had attempted to counter feminism as an attack on public morality. Anxieties about an uncertain economic future and the dislike of increasingly humanist values celebrated in schools were projected, by some parents, onto the education system, with the result that homeschooling came to be seen as the only option.

## Why homeschool?

*Many Christian parents are committed to educating their children at home because of their conviction that it is God's will for their family.*

*(in Apple 2001: 182)*

Hammons (2001) makes reference to the concerns of the right regarding the values being taught in schools and, also, to the contradictory liberal view that schools stifle creativity and are obsessed with standardized testing as the main reasons why people choose to homeschool. Romanowski (2001) summarizes the description provided by Van Galen (1988), which divides the homeschoolers into two broad groups:

- **ideologues** – often Christian, who believe that schools are no longer 'Christian enough'
- **pedagogues** – those people who think that schools offer poor teaching and do little to cater for individual learning needs

Research has shown that the greater parental involvement provided by homeschooling helps children reach their potential as learners (Simmons 1994 in Romanowski 2001) and also strengthens the relationship between them. Referring to the work of Van Galen (1988), Romanowski goes on to list positive self-esteem as an outcome of homeschooling, while also noting that the children are able to deal with multi-age relationships better than their contemporaries, because they are not segregated into year groups for much of their lives. Similarly, homeschooled children have the advantage that the curriculum can be changed to cater for their individual needs, and lesson length is not a 'given' that can't be altered. Of course, the children also receive far more individual attention compared to being just one of 30 in a class. Finally, the negative experiences of school can be avoided altogether, as competition and testing become less important. Interestingly, Meighan (1997) suggests that there do not seem to be issues of poor behaviour, so often reported in larger schools. Meighan also suggests that homeschoolers maintain that the happiness of the child is their main priority and this was evidenced in a study of homeschoolers in Canada in 1993 (in Meighan 1997: 13).

## Who homeschools?

Home schooling is often favoured by some religious fundamentalists, although it would be wrong to stereotype this growing movement. Some inner-city minorities have also seen fit to educate their children at home, as a rejection of the inadequate local schools in their area. Similarly, some parents of a liberal persuasion who dislike the over-emphasis on testing and labelling children according to a narrow means of assessment, have taken the decision to develop their own curriculum.

Although educational background has not been found to be as important a factor in the success of the home-educated as you might imagine, the majority of homeschoolers do appear to come from better educated families (Apple 2007), are better off financially and are more likely to be white. It is also interesting, but not surprising, to note that it is the mothers who carry out most of the teaching duties at home, which is, of course, frequently hard work (ibid.).

The main reason not to homeschool that no doubt first springs to mind, is the notion of socialization. Children learn to mix with a diverse social group through attending their local schools. This also exposes them to a range of ideas and viewpoints, which would be lacking if they were confined to the home. In school, they also acquire the skills of discussing ideas and interacting that are necessary for adult life. Another key factor, is the issue of resources; it would be difficult for any home to replicate the kind of facilities that most schools offer. Also, many parents do not feel that they have the requisite skills to teach at all, and they certainly lack the subject specialisms to cover the range of the curriculum. How many of us would be disciplined enough to resist the interruptions of the telephone, or visitors? For such a reason, Van Galen (1988) suggests that homeschooled pupils may lack the generic skills of time-management, collaborative group-working and organization. Finally, Jamieson (2008) makes the important point that children have rights too, and they deserve to have a high standard of education and to be able to mix with other children outside of the home.

To counter the negative arguments, research in the UK by Thomas in 1994 indicates that highly structured forms of learning are not, actually, necessary for children to become successful learners. At home, children can and do learn 'just by living' (Thomas 1994 in Meighan 1997: 14). There has also been much criticism of schools post-1988 that likens them to factories with children as products, whereas homeschoolers argue that their children are individuals who take part in real two-way communication. Indeed, some children are allowed to determine their own curriculum, a system referred to by Hammons (2001) as 'unschooling'. He goes on to comment that in reality, the 'otherwise' curriculum is more likely to be focused on study skills, critical thinking, independent learning and fostering a desire to learn in general, with an emphasis on more traditional subjects such as reading, writing, languages and higher level maths. Of course, the development of technology and the internet has made it possible for anyone with a computer and a phone line to access resources from all over the world. Moreover, it allows for the establishment of 'virtual communities' of homeschoolers to support each other.

## The impact of homeschooling on education and society in general

While studies of homeschool initiatives remain small (see Meighan 1997), many writers acknowledge that this is a fast-growing movement (Hammons 2001; Koetzsch 1997;

Meighan 1997; Apple 2001). Moreover, all agree that homeschooled young people continue to score highly in national tests in both the UK and the USA, a fact that does not seem to be dependent on the parents' own educational record, nor the children's previous record if they attended mainstream school. As a result, many homeschoolers are now being accepted into higher education (Wasley 2007). Indeed, some students have been very successful in gaining work placements in government, a fact that one author at least, Jamieson (2008), notes with concern. Could it be that this movement of approximately 3 per cent of the population is positioning itself to have a significant influence over future educational policy? Could homeschooling provide a blueprint for the future of all schools being 'de-schooled'? If this is a possibility, what role could other contexts in the community play in the education of its young people? Could teachers be completely replaced by mentors? (Ellis 1996 in Meighan 1997: 47).

While we can learn a great deal from the homeschooling movement, Apple (2001) advises caution. We can have sympathy with the criticisms that schools have become too bureaucratic and pay too little attention to parents' concerns, and that education is overly assessment driven (although many would disagree with the view that schools are leading the attack on family and religious values). If those parents who believe the latter, take the extreme action of withdrawing their children from state schooling into the 'safety' of the home, then it could lead us into a future world where children are brought up in homogeneous groups, isolated from the 'otherness' of the rest of society. Apple refers to this as 'the engineered pastoral', which is 'safe and predictable' (2001: 176). Such freedom of choice for some will inevitably not extend to all. If the state system ceases to exist, what would happen to the most disadvantaged groups in terms of educational experience? Consider, if people opt for homeschooling or even private schooling, should they continue to support the state system through their taxes? Alternatively, should groups of homeschoolers be entitled to access public funding to pay for materials that some of us might consider to be extreme, and without any accountability?

It seems certain that schools have to change in order to be able to produce learners who are confident and capable of managing life in the rapidly changing twenty-first century. Some models do, in fact, exist where state education manages to respond to public concerns while remaining committed to such principles as social justice. The current initiatives entitled 'The Futures Curriculum' and 'Building Schools for the Future' have a lot riding on them.

---

### Activity 8.4

- What do you think are the advantages and disadvantages of homeschooling?
- What kind of role could homeschooling have in an education system of the future?

# Summary

Traditional distinctions between formal, non-formal and informal education have focused on the learning that takes place. In this chapter we suggest that a variety of forms of learning are common to all educational experiences, and that a focus on the types of contexts in which learning and education take place can be more productive. In our focus on the 'formal' contexts in which learning can take place, we have explored the costs and benefits of a number of alternatives to traditional state provision. Our explorations of faith-based schooling and independent schooling, while evidencing choice for parents on the one hand and academic benefits for pupils on the other, mask the perpetuation of selection and the divisive effects of segregation based on class or religion. Similarly, our consideration of homeschooling provided an insight into the motivations behind, and consequences of, a loss of faith in, and total rejection of, other formal education systems.

Similarly, there is a warning for the state system that in trying both to imitate the private and push to provide greater diversification within the state sector that:

> . . . greater specialization and diversity between schools leads to wider gaps in attainment, and greater social inequality. For a Labour Government which came into office committed to 'high achievement for the many', that conclusion merits very serious attention. (Edwards 2002: 118)

## Key references

Apple, M. W. (2001), *Educating the 'Right' Way*. London: Routledge Falmer.
DCSF (2007), *Faith in the System*. Nottingham: DCSF Publications. Available at: http://www.dcsf.gov.uk/publications/faithinthesystem/pdfs/FaithInTheSystem.pdf
Meighan, R. (1997), *The Next Learning System: And Why Home-Schoolers Are Trailblazers*. Nottingham: Educational Heretics Press.
Walford, G. (2003), *British Private Schools: Research on Policy and Practice*. London: Woburn Press.

## Useful websites

www.education_otherwise.org
  Information and resources about homeschooling in the UK
www.isc.co.uk
  The Independent Schools Council website

# Learning in Places  9

While formal, institutionalized education and, consequently, schools, remain the main site for learning, they are increasingly, and particularly with respect to *lifelong learning*, no longer the only places where learning and training take place. 'Learning in places' is a termed coined by Bekerman et al. (2006) that serves to take the emphasis away from the debate about *formality* and *informality* in educational provision that we alluded to in Chapter 8, in order to focus on the actual contexts, other than our traditional notion of school, in which learning can take place. Thus, Bekerman et al. (2006) suggest that out of school settings such as museums, art galleries, theatres, the home, the workplace, the shopping mall and the internet, are all considered to be 'learning places'. These contexts offer a range of opportunities for learning, usually based firmly in the experiential tradition, and are utilized by a variety of learners from adults to children in schools and also those being homeschooled. Meighan (1997) regards such 'community' learning places as being essential to the future shape of education.

In this chapter we will consider three such contexts: museums, theatres and extended schools' initiatives. In so doing, we will provide an insight into what such diverse contexts can contribute to the 'learning society'.

# Museums, galleries and heritage sites

## Learning in museums, galleries and heritage sites
*By Suzanne Spicer*

Museums, galleries and heritage sites collect and conserve our heritage for future generations. One of their key roles is as centres of lifelong learning. Over the last couple of decades, museum learning has seen a fundamental shift from being known as 'education' and seen as a knowledge-based, structured output system with an institutional focus, to 'learning' a user-focused, enabling approach based on outcomes.

Today, museum learning is considered to be an integrated and holistic experience that encompasses emotions, feelings, skills, creativity and action. It is often unintentional and accidental and is social, creative and collaborative in nature. Therefore, no one model of learning is adopted but a hybrid of many, with the most popular being the constructivist, based on active meaning-making and the cultural model, with its multi-dimensional aspect.

This dynamic and changing understanding of learning in museums has addressed the new agendas of learning for empowerment and personalized learning. It values partnership working and considers that it is the responsibility of the whole organization to create a positive learning environment for its visitors. Maslow's hierarchy of needs, when applied to a museum, indicates that in order to inspire visitors to learn, organizations need to provide access to food, drink and toilet facilities; create a feeling of being safe; make visitors feel as if they belong and are welcomed; and recognize visitor contribution so they feel confident and valued. By enabling and facilitating learning, museums can, therefore, have a shared dialogue with their visitors.

To drive this change and place learning at the heart of all museums, galleries and heritage sites, the government body responsible for museums, libraries and archives – the Museums, Libraries and Archives Council – launched a quality framework based on outcomes, called 'Inspiring Learning for All'. This defines museum learning as:

> . . . a process of active engagement with experience. It is what people do when they want to make sense of the world. It may involve increase in skills, knowledge, understanding, values and capacity to reflect. Effective learning leads to change, development and the desire to learn more. (Based on the definition from Campaign for Learning)

The framework aims to create accessible museums that stimulate and support learning. It is based on four areas:

- people – providing more effective learning opportunities.
- places – creating inspiring and accessible learning environments.
- partnerships – building creative learning partnerships.
- policies, plans, performance – placing learning at the heart of the organization.

To measure the outcomes of change and understand how visitors learn in museums, a coding tool called the 'Generic Learning Outcomes' (GLOs) was devised by the Research Centre for Museums and Galleries at the University of Leicester. It provides a common language and a shared understanding across all museums, considers learning in its broadest sense, and puts the learner first. There are five GLOs:

- knowledge and understanding
- skills

- attitudes and values
- enjoyment, inspiration, creativity
- action, behaviour, progression

Museums can now demonstrate the impact they have on visitors and show their unique contribution to the learning agenda. More recently, evidence has shown that museums, galleries and heritage sites also have a social impact on communities, so the 'Inspiring Learning for All' approach has been used to create a 'Generic Social Outcomes' (GSOs) framework. Three GSOs have been identified:

- stronger and safer communities – supporting cultural diversity and identity, tackling crime, improving dialogue and understanding.
- health and well-being – encouraging healthy lifestyles, supporting care and recovery, supporting older people, helping young people make a positive contribution.
- strengthening public life – encouraging participation in local decision-making, building capacity in the Third Sector, providing public spaces, enabling community empowerment, responsive to community needs.

What do museums, galleries and heritage sites offer for formal and informal learners? Most organizations will provide some or all of the following events and activities for learners of all ages, depending on their collections and resources:

**Object handling** in which people are allowed to look at certain objects from the museum collection up close and often to touch them. On each of The Manchester Museum's monthly 'Big Saturday' family event days, object handling sessions are run that are linked to the event theme. Visitors can handle numerous items from the collection, including beetles, gemstones, rocks, and ancient Egyptian jewellery.

**Hands-on workshops** are run by many museums, galleries and heritage sites during weekends and school holidays. Many are drop-in and are suitable for all ages including under 5s. The Whitworth Art Gallery in Manchester holds 'Colourful Sundays' throughout the year when visitors, particularly families, can take part in creative workshops run by artists and staff.

**Taught sessions** are often provided for schools and are usually directly related to the National Curriculum. Such sessions are led by museum staff and involve practical hands-on activities. They are usually based in a classroom or in galleries. At the Museum of Science and Industry (MOSI) in Manchester, 'Who's Afraid of the Dark' is a one-hour taught session aimed at Key Stage 1 children. It uses the story of 'Plop the Owl' to teach children about electric circuits. Teachers are encouraged to visit the Electricity Gallery with their children to link the session to the museum's collection.

**Shows and demonstrations** are often found at heritage sites and museums that have working historic machinery. In MOSI's Power Hall Gallery, various working steam engines are demonstrated every day by staff, some of which use costumed characters such as James Watt, or provide interactive presentations for children such as 'Engineer Eric' and 'Forgetful Fireman Fred'.

**Talks, tours and lectures** are offered by many organizations as well as talk/lecture programmes mainly for older audiences. More recently, debates have been held on ethical and scientific topics allowing visitors to question different experts on their opinions. The Manchester City Art Gallery's free tour for groups, entitled the 'Manchester Tour', explores the artists, artworks and decorative objects related to the history of Manchester from the eighteenth century to today.

**Courses for teachers and ITT students** are provided by many museums, galleries and heritage sites. Some offer free preliminary visits and the opportunity to speak to staff, while others provide organised INSET sessions or bespoke days for individual schools. The Whitworth Art Gallery provides free professional development events for teachers on developing their skills and knowledge in art and design, based round the items in the Gallery's collection.

⇨

> **Learning in museums, galleries and heritage sites—cont'd**
>
> **Outreach** involves taking activities and objects off-site to different audiences. Some organizations provide handling-objects for loan, others provide staff to give talks for different community groups, and some run activities at community events. MOSI works with various community groups on creating and developing exhibitions for their dedicated Community Exhibition Gallery. All exhibitions are based on, or use, objects from both the museum's collection and from the communities themselves.
>
> *Suzanne was formerly the Learning Manager at the Museum of Science and Industry, Manchester, and is now Manchester Beacon Project Manager.*

. . . learning in museums is not a-historical, a-political, taking place in a void. It is substantially affected, both in the policies and in the practices employed, by the wider political, economic and educational, policy agendas. (Grek 2005: 1)

While the value of using museums for educational purposes is self-evident, it must be remembered that museums, like more formal educational contexts, are not socially and culturally neutral institutions. Museums can be viewed as 'cultural creations or cultural institutions' that simply reflect the culture of the society in which they exist. Thus, museum exhibitions, and also their educational programmes, promote understandings that are influenced by this cultural context, therefore, serving to perpetuate certain cultural norms and practice (Bekerman et al. 2006). Grek also refers to Bourdieu's work in which he argues that museum visiting is still largely a recreation of the well-educated and that to engage in the world of museums 'requires a willingness to "play the game of art"' (2004: 3). However, she also cites Gramsci as having put forward a persuasive argument that museums, theatres and leisure centres, for example, have an important role to play in 'shaping self and group identities and distinguishing different conceptions of community and belonging', which can, if they decide to adopt the challenge, be emancipatory rather than a simple telling of the status quo (in Grek 2004: 4).

Learning places such as museums, therefore, have a potentially powerful function, which is to help create a new 'unified and humanistic' culture. Grek (2004) also adapts Gramsci's arguments about education generally, and calls for a new examination of the aims and values of museums and other such contexts, their mission statements and, therefore, of their educational programmes.

# Theatre as education

Drama has been a valuable learning medium for centuries and has been a popular subject within the school curriculum for decades. 'Theatre as education' is concerned with the use of theatre as a site for learning, i.e. a 'learning place'. While the majority of research has been focused on 'formal learning', that is, drama teaching within the school curriculum, there has been a recognition that the use of 'theatre as education' can provide a place for valuable informal learning outside of traditional school activities (James 2005: 8). James also points out that:

> . . . what is of fundamental importance . . . is the art form . . . the theatre and its application outside of a formal education setting. What theatre offers uniquely as an art form is a level of involvement that draws directly on the experiences, the character, the very persona of the participant. (ibid.: 9)

## Theatre 'in' education

*TiE is not a traditional teaching process: its value is as a medium of personal contact that offers knowledge of social problems through involving pupils in a process through which they learn critical skills in assessing social issues and the impact of their decisions on other people's lives.*

*(Sextou 2003: 186)*

There are a number of ways of engaging children, young people and even adults in the process of learning through drama that operate in partnership with different and distinctive groups. Most teachers would probably think first of 'Theatre in Education' (TiE) groups, whose origin dates back to the 1960s in England. The emphasis here is on education rather than theatre as such, and the aim would be to be to bring about positive and meaningful experiences for children who get involved in the dramatic process through workshops and interactive sessions, usually following a performance in the school. The scripts are frequently written by the actor-teachers themselves, and arise out of a concern about a particular issue, such as asylum seekers or child protection. The topics are usually linked directly to subjects within the curriculum and often the actors are in role throughout and aim to create greater understanding of societal issues.

In the late 1990s, many TiE companies turned away from their traditional roots, forced in the main by financial imperatives, and started to focus on 'young people's theatre' (Sextou 2003: 180). As such, they provide professional theatre for children and young people that includes a diversity of programmes such as arts events, theatre activities and professional theatre productions, in a variety of venues. As a result, there has been a diversification of the types of theatre education provided for young people (ibid.: 181) that includes:

- young people's theatre
- Theatre in Education
- children's theatre
- educational theatre
- theatre in schools
- theatre workshops

What about the future of TiE? Sextou suggest that if TiE is to survive then it 'must not abandon its broad principles, central to which is social learning through participatory theatre in interactive programmes for young people in schools' (2003: 184).

## Community theatre

Community theatre groups work in a similar way to TiE, but their audience includes adults, often those who are disadvantaged. The aim of this form of education is to help foster greater social cohesion and equality by empowering their participants; workshops can be supplemented by training programmes. Of course, part of the attraction of using theatre as a teaching medium is going out of the school, college or home and visiting the theatre itself. Many regional theatres have an education department, which may be staffed by former teachers and which offer a variety of activities for children and young people. The emphasis is not on theatre skills but on content, sometimes written by the staff themselves, and sometimes based on existing material. The play itself is the key, not necessarily the issue within the play. Visits can include a follow-up workshop and backstage tour (Teachernet 2008).

Such a programme is provided by the Royal Exchange Theatre in Manchester, which develops partnerships with schools, community groups, practitioners and other arts organizations. The Education department aims to reflect the diversity of the theatre's environment and the different ethnicities represented in Greater Manchester. One example is a recent collaboration, the Muslim-Jewish Youth Theatre, a project that ran for a number of weeks culminating in a presentation. The aim was to encourage understanding, communication and peace. Other projects have been for young offenders and young people on probation; outcomes included improved self-esteem and greater confidence for the individuals involved (visit www.royalexchange.org for more information).

Community theatre initiatives emphasize the socializing aspects of education and the unifying experience of collaboration on a creative project. The importance of the unique community-building design is central to the mission of the theatre, and the desire to attract those social groups who would not necessarily feel a link with the arts. In this way, theatres and also other learning places, like museums, have a claim to promoting social inclusion (Grek 2004). However, just as in the past, when theatre in education was often criticized for being 'leftist and propagandist' (Sextou 2003), could such initiatives now, similarly, be accused of having a hidden agenda of social control?

---

### Activity 9.1

What do you think the main aims of theatre and museum education should be? Do you agree that behind the intrinsic aims published in the mission statements of most museums and TiE initiatives, there is now a hidden agenda of attempting to re-skill people through their participation in the arts, as instrumentalism in disguise? Would that be a bad thing?

# Extended schools

*An extended school maximises the curricular learning of its pupils by promoting their overall development and by ensuring that the family and community contexts within which they live are as supportive of learning as possible.*

*(Cummings et al. 2004 in Smith 2004, 2005: 9)*

An 'extended school' is one that can 'provide a range of services and activities, often beyond the school day, to help meet the needs of children, their families and the wider community' (DfES 2005: 7). In this context, the school itself, outside of 'normal' school hours, becomes an alternative 'learning place' for all members of the community. According to Smith (2004, 2005) the notion of 'extended schooling' in England was borrowed from the American concept of 'full service schools', where community facilities for health and welfare and many other community activities are often physically located within schools and occur alongside traditional schooling. In 2002, following the emergence of new community schools in Scotland, the government launched the Extended Schools initiative in England (see DfES 2002). The purpose of this initiative was to extend the role of schools within the community so that schools:

- provide greater access for pupils, families and the wider community during and beyond the school day, before and after school hours, at weekends and during school holidays
- provide activities aimed particularly at vulnerable groups in areas of deprivation and/or where services are limited
- promote community cohesion by building links with the wider community through the provision of services to communities and make a contribution to neighbourhood renewal
- have a positive effect on educational standards

*(Adapted from Smith 2004, 2005: 3)*

Many schools have been slow to adapt to the changes proposed by the Extended Schools initiatives, and few have adopted the 'full service model' that is the government's ideal, although many are working towards such a model. Most activities that form part of extended school provision tend to be focused on learning and are representative of the raft of 'out of school' learning activities that schools provided in the past. Such activities include breakfast and after school clubs, family and adult education programmes, childcare and community use of school facilities, for example sports facilities and libraries (Cummings et al. 2004 and Wilkin et al. 2003, both cited in Smith 2004, 2005: 4, 6).

## Issues

Smith (2004) highlights a number of issues that arise from the notion of extended schools and that could possibly impact on the success of such projects:

- Extended schools may become stigmatized as being schools for 'problem families'.
- Schools focus largely on 'out of school' educational provision for their own pupils and do not actually engage in a significant amount of true 'community education'.

- The introduction of parental choice and the development of specialist schools and academies have meant that more pupils, particularly at secondary level, travel great distances to school. As a consequence, schools are, in many cases, no longer 'local' to the communities that they are supposed to serve.
- The use of a 'deficit or medical' model when dealing with issues in the local communities attached to schools. In this way the individuals within the community are 'pathologized' and the focus of actions and initiatives is on providing 'preventions or cures' for the problems and behaviours, rather than on the provision of quality educational experiences.
- Lack of collaboration with other agencies that are an integral part of the extended school ethos.
- The remodelling of the school workforce has resulted in teachers being freed from other duties in order to focus on teaching. Their role within an extended school context, however, remains unclear.

While there are obviously issues and problems associated with such a wide ranging reconceptualization of the role and functioning of the school within a community setting, there are numerous examples of individual success among extended school initiatives. The provision of one such initiative, 'Playing for Success', is detailed in the next section.

---

### Playing for Success

*By Lois Gyves*

Playing for Success is a national government initiative that was established in 1997 by the DfES in partnership with local authorities and the Football Association Premier League. Since then it has expanded to include a wider range of professional sports. The scheme provides out-of-school hours Study Support provision for 9–14 year olds in centres based in sports venues. The focus is to provide innovative learning opportunities to raise standards in literacy, numeracy, ICT and promote self-esteem and confidence in learning using the medium and environment of sport to foster children's motivation.

Nationally, Playing for Success has expanded and developed from three venues in 1997 to over 160 centres nationwide. There are three PfS centres in Manchester, two are partnered with Manchester City Football Club, one at the MCFC stadium and one at the Platt Lane Complex; the third is partnered with Sale Harriers Athletic Club in Wythenshawe. Over 1000 pupils each year participate in a ten-week after-school programme of activities, which they attend on a voluntary basis. The centres work closely with the school staff who target pupils they feel will benefit the most from the programme.

The ethos of the centres is to provide a high quality Study Support experience to develop positive attitudes to learning, in an environment where the children feel valued and inspired to improve and develop their skills. All the sessions are delivered by qualified teachers, and the children are given additional support from a team of learning mentors. The majority of the mentors are young people studying at local HE and FE colleges and universities. The mentors are positive role models encouraging attitudes to 'aim high' and the ethos of lifelong learning. PfS Manchester also works with a variety of agencies, services and organizations to support the delivery of a range of other learning activities both out-of-school hours and during curriculum time.

Research into the effectiveness of PfS in terms of raising pupils' performance in National Curriculum Assessments indicates clearly that pupils do gain significantly from attending the Study Support centres (Sharp et al. 1999, 2001, 2002, 2003 in Sharp et al. 2007: 1). However, statistical data regarding pupils' long-term gains is inconclusive. Qualitative data points to the fact that underachieving young people are given a new and valuable opportunity, but stresses the importance of students being recognized for their efforts and successes and, in particular, that there is continuing support after their attendance at the project has come to an end. The most successful centres did put in place specific strategies for maximizing learner support and, thus, enabling the young people to transfer their achievements to the school setting. This requires strong partnerships between the centres, schools and other related organizations. The scheme seems to be particularly effective with lower-attaining pupils who should, possibly, be given priority for places. Sharing good practice is, of course, essential and monitoring long-term impact is recommended locally and regionally.

There is no doubt, however, that 'the government, local authorities and sponsors should continue to support PfS' (Sharp et al. 2007: 2), while end of term celebration events provide a valuable forum for many young people to be publicly rewarded for their efforts, in some cases, for the first time in their school careers. Schools must continue to capitalize on this success.

*Lois is the Co-ordinator for Playing for Success in Manchester.*

---

### Activity 9.2
### The new 'place' for learning?

The invention of the World Wide Web has had a significant effect on all our lives. In particular, the use of so called 'People Net' resources are on the increase. Consider how the use of the following 'People Net' resources, could impact on education as a new 'learning place':

- wikis
- folksonomies
- YouTube
- Google
- Facebook and Bebo
- Second Life

# Summary

Smith points out that 'within policy debates a common differentiation has been made between different forms of provision. Informal, non-formal and formal programmes have been viewed as very different' (1999: 1). However, he goes on to cite Coffield, who suggests that such forms of learning:

> . . . should no longer be regarded as an inferior form of learning whose main purpose is to act as a precursor of formal learning; it needs to be seen as fundamental, necessary and valuable in its own right. (Coffield 2000: 8 in Smith 1999: 1)

In this chapter we have argued just that: that learning is learning whether the context is formal or non-formal. We have, therefore, focused on the contexts in which learning, in all forms, can take place. Thus we have explored the potential for museums, theatres and the school outside of normal school hours, to act as a 'learning place'.

## Key references

Hooper-Greenhill, E. (2007), *Museums and Education: Purpose, Pedagogy, Performance*. London: Routledge.

Bekerman, Z., Burbules, N. C. and Silberman Keller, D. (2006), *Learning in Places: The Informal Education Reader*. New York: Peter Lang.

## Useful websites

www.teachernet.gov.uk
   The education site for teachers and school managers for information on extended schools initiatives
www.infed.org
   The online encyclopaedia and archives of informal education
www.mla.gov.uk
   The Museums, Libraries and Archives Council's website
www.inspiringlearningforall.gov.uk
   Information and resources related to the Inspiring Learning for All Framework

# Alternative Education

## Alternative education

*Our aim is to ensure that every child and young person has the opportunity to fulfil their potential and no child slips through the net.*

*(Every Child Matters: Next Steps 2004: 5)*

According to Rix and Twining, the standards, choice and inclusion agendas, together with new developments in ICT, have resulted in 'creating diversity of educational provision to meet the full range of needs presented by learners' (2007: 329). These agendas have not only resulted in increasing diversity within traditional educational provision, but also in the so-called 'alternative' provision. Although there is no commonly accepted definition of 'alternative education', it is generally taken to refer to a variety of environments, contexts and initiatives that fall outside the traditional system (Aron 2003).

Initially, the term 'alternative education' was linked with movements such as the Free School Movement in America and Education Otherwise, that is, with movements that were set up in opposition to traditional school systems. However, alternative education has increasingly become synonymous with the education of children who do not do well in traditional contexts, who have been left behind or excluded due their behaviour or actions. As a consequence, alternative education programmes have often been associated with notions of 'discipline' and viewed as 'dumping grounds' for problem pupils. However, many alternative education programmes are now being viewed in a more positive light. Alternative education is increasingly being seen as innovative and creative and a viable means of providing ways of connecting disaffected pupils with main stream education. As a result, many traditional schools are incorporating aspects of alternative education into their provision (ibid.).

> Research has shown the link between exclusion from school and involvement in offending and other antisocial behaviours. Whilst the government is striving to reduce the number of young people out of school in general, and those excluded from school in particular, the quality and effectiveness of alternative educational provision is of importance, if further social exclusion and possible drift into crime is to be averted. (Kendall et al. 2003: 3)

A number of researchers have attempted to produce a typology of educational provision that enables reference to be made to alternative educational provision (see Aron, 2003: 25; Raywid 1998; Rix and Twining 2007: 332). Our discussions of the dimensions of alternative educational provision will therefore be framed by some of the dimensions of the educational programmes typology they propose.

## Who is it for?

There is a growing number of young people who do not attend school for a variety of reasons. Such children come from a diversity of backgrounds and are challenged by a wide range of complex problems. They include children who have:

- long-term medical or emotional problems
- school phobia
- been excluded by their mainstream school
- have committed an offence
- are pregnant or are young mothers
- have run away from home
- come from traveller, asylum or refugee families
- come from a homeless family or live in a women's refuge
- are a young carer
- have dropped out of school
- are 'looked-after children'

While many of these children may be homeschooled or find themselves in alternative educational provision, there are 10,000 such children that are actually 'missing' completely from all forms of education, having never been registered for school or having been lost from the school rolls (Ofsted 2004). Such children not only miss out on their right to an education, but are at a greater risk from:

- physical harm
- sexual abuse
- being involved in crime

There are currently approximately 70,000 pupils in alternative education at any one time in England, with up to 135,000 young people spending some time in an alternative provision in the course of a year. The vast majority of these children have some form of special educational need (DCSF 2008). The largest proportion of children in alternative provision (56 per cent) are children who are ill, hospitalized, suffering from a long-term medical condition or are pregnant. Overall, these groups include slightly more girls than boys (DfES and TNS 2003). A slightly smaller percentage of pupils receiving alternative education are either permanently excluded from school or are at risk of exclusion. The majority of pupils who are excluded from school are boys (60 per cent), the majority of which (91 per cent) are between the ages of 11 and 15 (DCSF 2008). LEAs also have to provide for the needs of children who have emotional and behavioural difficulties (EBD). Most children with EBD (51 per cent) are placed in maintained mainstream schools or in maintained special schools (30 per cent), while a small percentage (7 per cent) receive alternative provision. Schools, however, are often reluctant to reintegrate such pupils into mainstream education, a fact that is exacerbated by a shortage of places. There are also concerns over the ability of schools to deal with such pupils' difficulties (DfES and TNS 2003).

## Where does it take place and who provides it?

Alternative education provision can take on a variety of forms, some of which take place within mainstream schools, some within alternative school settings and some within non-school, formal settings (Rix and Twining 2007: 332). Alternative educational provision includes:

- **that provided directly by LEAs**:
  o Pupil Referral Units PRUs
  o home tuition
  o hospital schools
  o special units for pregnant teenagers or young mothers
  o behaviour support units
- **augmented support in mainstream schools**:
  o learning support units
  o in-school units for pupils with SEN
  o extended work experience
  o flexibility in the 14–16 programme
  o links with FE, Connexions and Social Services provision
- **that provided by other organizations**:
  o private residential day care
  o secure units

○ independent schools
○ Social Services Centres and Residential Units with educational provision
○ therapeutic units
○ Asylum Centres

Many alternative education programmes are short term or provided alongside normal schooling. For example, they might provide a short-term bridge between a period of exclusion or absence from mainstream education and the pupil's return, or offer accelerated learning towards a specific goal. Other programmes are a more permanent alternative to mainstream schooling, providing regular tuition or occupational training. In general, the funding for alternative education is provided by LEAs, however, other funding comes from a variety of sources including, for example, private funding, the Children's Fund and the European Social Fund.

## What is it for?

As well as taking a number of forms, alternative education has a variety of purposes, which include:

- completing academic qualifications
- preparing individuals for their career
- discipline or behaviour modification
- enabling the transition between exclusion and mainstream education

Alternative education, therefore, provides pupils with access not only to mainstream education opportunities, but to a more flexible curriculum that can include access to vocational training and specialist therapies dependent on the individual pupil's learning needs. In the following sections we will explore the features of some of the main forms of alternative education.

# Pupil referral units

The term Pupil Referral Unit (PRU) refers to a local authority run alternative school provision for excluded pupils. The first PRUs were set up in 1993, mainly as short stay centres. There are now 450 PRUs in England catering for 25,000 pupils, which is approximately one third of the pupils in alternative educational provision (DCSF 2008). As we have already seen, the vast majority of pupils who are excluded from schools are boys aged 11–15. However, a disproportionate number of those excluded are also from minority ethnic backgrounds. In particular, black Caribbean pupils are far more likely to be excluded than other social groups, three times more likely than white pupils and fourteen times more likely than pupils of Indian heritage (DfES and TNS 2003). Pupils with special needs and those who have been in local authority care are also overrepresented in the numbers of exclusions.

Exclusions are very rarely overturned and only a small percentage of excluded children return to school (DCSF 2008).

Schools are legally allowed to exclude pupils on a temporary (fixed-term) basis, or a permanent basis if a child's behaviour is deemed serious enough. Only the headteacher can actually exclude a pupil, and no child can be excluded on a fixed-term basis for more than 45 days in any one year. If a child is excluded permanently, the governing body must review the headteacher's decision and the parent can appeal to an independent panel. From day six of the exclusion, the local authority must provide full-time alternative education (Directgov.co.uk 2008), however, studies reveal that some authorities can take up to nine months to find alternative provision, and that 42 per cent of excludees surveyed felt that no one encouraged them back into education (The Prince's Trust 2002).

A study of the family background of excluded children found that they are far more likely to come from single parent households, with only one in four living with both parents, the respondents commenting that their parents showed little interest in their school progress and that they were not subject to discipline at home. Pupils also reported a lack of role-models in their lives. Over half of children who had been in local authority care who were surveyed in the research had been excluded from school, and many of the respondents had poor levels of basic skills (The Prince's Trust 2002). An earlier study by the Social Exclusion Unit (1998) found that excludees have complex problems that include low aspirations and a peer/family culture that does not value education. The problems of exclusion, however, do not lie only with the children and their families. Other factors, such as large, impersonal schools where teachers do not get to know children well, may also contribute (Ofsted 2006).

When a pupil is excluded permanently from school, we have seen that the authorities have to provide an alternative. This can be at another local school, through a process known, in some areas, as 'Managed Moves'. Schools can enter into agreements so that they will accept each other's pupils, who may also be accompanied by a support worker and a 'Personal Education Plan'. Those children whose behaviour is deemed too challenging for a mainstream school, however, may be sent to a special school for students with behavioural and/or social difficulties. These take in a smaller number of students and have a higher staff/pupil ratio so that classes can be kept to a manageable size, with children receiving more individual support. More recently, pupils have been placed in PRUs that also cater for children who need a lot of support and from where older students may be sent to part-time work experience, or vocational courses in an FE college. Interestingly, students report favourably about their experiences in a PRU, commenting that they were given the help they needed. They also preferred the less authoritarian environment, were more willing to learn, enjoyed learning and wanted to continue with their education in the future (The Prince's Trust 2002; Kendall et al. 2003).

Evans (2007) provides a snapshot of one school for 72 pupils aged 5–16, all of whom have been excluded from their previous schools. The school uses the latest technology to develop digital creativity in the pupils, encouraging group learning and social skills. The children are allowed to take laptops home, and this trust has led to improved attendance and attainment. Success with technology helps to empower the children, according to the headteacher, and out of this comes a new relationship with learning.

> I don't think any of these kids I work with chose the start in life they got. And we can ameliorate that start by supplying good kit and interesting learning environments. Society gets the children it deserves; our children represent us. (D'Abbro 2007 in Evans 2007)

Not all education offered by PRUs and special schools is so successful. Sadly, they are often 'more likely to reinforce your belief that you're ineducable and not cut out for "normal" society'. While there are some extremely good units, the majority have been found by Ofsted to be institutions in which 'children are poorly served'. The alternative to a PRU is getting a few hours a week of 'home tuition' (Klein 2000: 9).

Klein (2000) highlights a number of studies that point to the link between being excluded from school and getting involved in crime, commenting on one PRU in London where 65 per cent of pupils have had contact with the police. It should not be surprising, therefore, that when we look at our next context in this section, we can see that many of the students who find themselves in prison or young offender institutions, have had a poor experience of education in school and have frequently been rejected by the mainstream schools they attended.

---

### Activity 10.1

- For what reasons should students be excluded from school?
- What can schools do to reduce the number of exclusions?
- What do you think should be the aims of a PRU?

---

# Prison education

A context that is often forgotten in relation to the provision of education is that of prisons and youth offender institutions, which cater for large groups of people. In July 2008, for example, 2,938 young people were in custody, of which 2,480 were in young offender institutions and were between 10 and 17 years of age. A further 240 were held in secure training centres and 218 in secure children's homes (Youth Justice Board 2008). Boys make up the majority of this group, only 206 girls were in prison in 2008. With respect to adults, there were 83,518 people in prison in September 2008, the vast majority of whom are men. There are also disproportionate numbers of certain social groups in prisons, including 'ethnic minorities, the poor, the dispossessed and the rebellious' (Devine 2007: 2). Over half of offenders have been unemployed before being sentenced, and few have the requisite knowledge and skills to enable them to gain employment when they are released (Home Office 2004 in Lohmann-Hancock 2006: 4). Education is therefore a vital part of the rehabilitation programme for both young offenders and adult prisoners.

## Organization

Learning and Skills for offenders in custody have been delivered by a number of training providers who have a contract with the Prison Service, while vocational training is delivered by Instructional Officers who are employed by the Prison Service. Both services have been funded from the Offenders' Learning and Skills Unit, under the Learning and Skills Council since August 2005. Later the service became known as the 'Offenders' Learning and Skills Service', although this is set to change again in 2009 (Jackson 2007). Prisons are actually the largest adult basic skills providers in the country, with around 50,000 awards being gained each year, although mostly below level three (The Centre for Crime and Justice Studies 2005). What is more, 'learning provision has been neglected until fairly recently, many would say scandalously so' (Adult Learning Inspectorate 2006: 14 in Jackson 2007: 1).

## Aims of prison education

*. . . while punishment will always be the primary aim of the criminal justice system, the Government is determined to do more to turn offenders away from crime and into work, improving their skills and encouraging them to lead productive lives.*

*(DIUS 2008)*

The 'Offenders' Learning Journey', produced by the government in 2004, stated very clearly that there are two aims for 'offender management'. One was to provide safe and well-ordered establishments. The other was to reduce the risk of reoffending. Providing education for offenders was seen to have a bearing on both these goals. It was set out that offenders were to have access to education and training, according to their need, so that they could gain skills and qualifications in order to be able to keep a job. It is clear from these statements that the dominant philosophy governing prison education is instrumental. According to Devine (2007), prisons in the UK are seen as potential contributors to the workforce, they could be perceived as 'training' institutions, whose inmates have a role to play in the nation's economy.

The 'Offenders' Learning Journey' also states that one of the main aims of the prison education service is to provide a focus on basic and key skills as well as vocational skills, and that the targets for inspection should emphasize the importance of learning and employability outcomes for offenders and entering sustainable employment. In order to achieve a target of at least 90 per cent of young offenders in suitable full-time education, training or employment by the end of their sentence, 90 per cent of young offenders receive between

25 and 30 hours a week of education, training and development. All young people entering secure facilities are tested for literacy and numeracy and are helped to increase their skills by one level. Each young person is provided with an individual training plan, which is regularly reviewed. These actions are predicated on the belief that 'engagement in education and training and acquiring skills for employability is regarded as one of the most important contributory factors towards achieving . . . the aim of reducing re-offending' (Braggins and Talbot 2005: 3).

According to Jackson (2007) there are contradictory perspectives at the core of the stated aims of prison education that are difficult to reconcile. One is idealistic and represents the view that prison education is valuable in itself, and the other view is that prison education actually has little impact on reducing reoffending.

---

### Activity 10.2

What do you think the aims of prison education should be?

You may like to consider whether prisoners should have access to education at all or whether education should be seen as a luxury and, therefore, denied to those who break the law.

---

## Influences and structure

There is a range of age groups catered for in youth offenders' institutions. The curriculum is necessarily influenced by the National Curriculum for those young people under the school leaving age. Every Child Matters also has sections relating to the rights of young people in terms of their educational outcomes, however, interestingly the Special Needs Code of Practice does not apply to those in custody. Recent changes to the 14–19 curriculum will also have a major impact on the opportunities offered to juvenile offenders. As we have seen, for older inmates, there is a focus on skills and more vocationally oriented work.

People coming before the courts, whether juvenile or adult, tend to have very low levels of education; as many as 60 per cent having poor literacy skills, and up to 75 per cent having poor numeracy skills (Uden 2004 in Jackson 2007). Many young offenders have no qualifications at all (52 per cent of men and 75 per cent of women compared with 15 per cent of the general population). Of course, by focusing on basic skills in order to redress this situation, the government has been accused of using the prison population to help reach literacy and numeracy targets. Also, as a consequence of such a narrow focus, Jackson (2007) argues that other deserving areas of the curriculum, such as higher level skills and personal development, are being squeezed out. The resulting curriculum offer can seem very dry and not necessarily at a high enough level to impact on offenders' employment prospects.

## The formal curriculum

The culture in prisons has been to regard education as something that takes place inside the classrooms where prisoners are allowed to spend certain parts of the day, and this attitude is slow to change. However, Braggins and Talbot (2005) suggest that this formal learning is supplemented by a range of other opportunities such as 'homework' activities carried out in cells, vocational training run by civilian prison staff, workshop training, gymnastics qualifications, NVQs achieved through working in such areas as the prison kitchen, and peer/officer mentoring schemes.

## The informal curriculum

Over and above these overt and structured learning opportunities, there are also more informal activities. PSHE usually falls into this category, according to prison officers interviewed by Braggins and Talbot (2005), as do quizzes and induction and pre-release courses provided by the prison officers themselves.

## The hidden curriculum

In prisons and youth offender institutions, as in schools, there is inevitably an influence that pervades all the interactions that take place within their confines. The pressure of this 'hidden curriculum' is such that often the only learning that is really reinforced is simply how to become a more skilled criminal. Networks can be established that provide opportunities upon release that enable the prisoner to return to their previous life with renewed energy. Wilson describes prisons as overcrowded 'universities of crime' (2002 in Jackson 2007: 5). Jackson (2007) suggests that perhaps the main aim of prison education could be to help prisoners create a new identity for themselves, such as that of 'student' or 'learner' as opposed to only identifying themselves as 'offender'. This would involve greater emphasis on courses that encouraged the development of positive self-esteem, with the support of mentoring programmes and even the possibility of allowing inmates to teach others. Are prisons capable of becoming 'learning communities' (ibid.) and 'is a prison context any different from other adult learning contexts' (Sheridan 2006: 19 in Jackson 2007: 3)?

## Issues

Behind all the statistics and comments we have been considering in this section, lies the larger question of what prison itself is for. Is it for rehabilitation or is it simply a system of punishing those who see themselves as being outside the law? If so, are prisons part of a process of 'normalizing' those members of society in order to render them harmless to the majority (Jackson 2007)? Is education central, therefore, to that process of passing on society's norms and values to this captive audience?

We have considered elsewhere in this book that education can be regarded as a human right, and it can be argued that prisoners deserve that right no less than anyone else. However, if we have decided that no one should be coerced into being educated, then shouldn't prisoners have the right to refuse educational opportunities too (Devine 2007)? Could it be true that education can be used to disguise the punishment aspect of imprisonment? Furthermore, if we have associated education with the notion of freedom, can inmates become free students able to choose to take part in, and develop respect for, the learning process? It is likely that many offenders, both young and old, have carried with them into custody old attitudes towards education that they acquired in school, and therefore do not see it as having any intrinsic worth. 'What's the point? I didn't learn anything really useful at school. So why start learning now?' (Lohmann-Hancock 2007: 16).

As education was seen as something that was 'done' to them and irrelevant, a need to learn must first be established if inmates are to redefine themselves as successful learners. Lohmann-Hancock (2007) suggests that by the time they reach prison, many offenders have realized that they were not perceived as having any value by schools or society in general. Certainly, prison educators have to behave differently in order to re-establish a connection with their students. Flexibility and honesty are central to this process. They need to understand how offender learners differ from other teenage and adult education groups and how they may have previously experienced the school process (ibid. 2007: 11).

Lohmann-Hancock argues that an 'interactionist rehabilitative model' (2007: 11) offers a way forward. This would mean taking into account the offenders' early experiences of education and how the environment and their interactions with that environment have influenced those experiences and shaped their attitude towards learning. An offender must be guided towards a redefining of themselves and a fundamental change in the way they view the whole educational process if prison education systems are to be truly successful. Otherwise, all that they can achieve is to mitigate against the way that prisons positively encourage reoffending (Martinson 1974 in Devine 2007) and help to make the prison regime itself more humane.

---

### Activity 10.3

Do you agree that the education of prisoners is fundamental to a democracy, or should prisoners be forced to do work that contributes to the economic success of the country?

   You will find it helpful to look back to the first section where we discussed the aims and purposes of education and consider how these relate to prison education.

## Working with young offenders

*By Derek Wolland*

The inmates vary quite widely in their abilities, though the majority are at the lower end of the educational spectrum. The majority will have had many problems in mainstream education, frequently
being excluded from their school at an early age due to their aberrant behaviour. They frequently
have no male figure as a role model. They can be members of gangs on the outside, dealing in drugs
and committing robbery. The range of crimes committed covers the full spectrum, including murder
and rape.

Working with these students requires patience, consistency and a strong sense of self. Any weak-
nesses will be seized upon and ruthlessly exploited by the lads. This is a form of entertainment for
them. It helps pass the time, which drags in prison. Gaining the trust of the students is therefore
something of a baptism of fire. If you can think on your feet and have a good sense of humour, you
can enjoy the work. However, if you are rigid in your thinking and feel you must win every little con-
frontation, you will wear yourself out. Controlling behaviour is a matter of respect. You treat your
students as responsible people even when you know they are not. You must insist on being treated
with respect yourself, and you must treat the students fairly and with consistency. These students
have a heightened sense of grievance. Rudeness and aggression are par for the course. Of course,
not all students are rude and aggressive, but most classes will contain at least one or two who are.
Bearing in mind that most of these students have been the most disruptive and troublesome at
their schools, their educational experience is mostly negative, therefore, positive encouragement is
a teacher's best tool.

*Derek is a prison education officer in a young offender institution.*

# Hospital education

If a child is too ill to attend school, the local authority has to provide them with as normal
an education as possible until they are well enough to be integrated back into an appropriate
school. This may mean working with a tutor at home, and if so, the children are entitled to
support from a tutor for approximately five hours a week. However, for many children suffering long-term illness, their education may also involve attending an educational provision within a hospital itself, a so-called hospital school, which should be 'of similar quality'
to that available in mainstream schools (Directgov.co.uk 2008).

A hospital education service, therefore, aims to provide continuity of educational experience for pupils whose medical needs mean that they are unable to continue with their previous schooling. The staff try to ensure that there is minimum disruption to the child's
education, and work in partnership with not only parents and teachers, but relevant medical personnel. The aims of such a service include making sure, where possible, that children in their care have access to the National Curriculum. Another aim is to help the child
integrate back into the mainstream provision when and if they are ready. Examinations can
also be taken in special centres if appropriate.

Children who are entitled to access such a service are usually referred by a senior medical officer or consultant, and are children who are likely to be absent from school for significant periods of time on account of poor health, or children who have serious mental health problems. Even children as young as 5 can fall into this category (Bristol Children and Young People's Service 2008). The benefits of being able to access such a service will include:

- trying to ensure that children do not miss out on education any more than is necessary
- being able to provide a small therapeutic environment that will best suit the child's needs
- having a range of practitioners available to respond to a child's complex needs

Most hospital education services will see their role as helping to rebuild a child's self-esteem and helping them overcome physical or emotional difficulties. Because these children have been away from their peers for significant periods of time, they may have feelings of isolation and negativity, which may be displayed as difficult behaviour. Work on interpersonal skills may be an important addition to a general academic programme as children learn to cope with the difficulties a chronic illness may cause on a long-term basis. The ultimate goal will be to enable children to engage with education as positively as possible, wherever that may be. During the consultation process, before drawing up the statutory guidance on access to education for such children and young people, it was noted that they faced numerous barriers when trying to continue with their education, such as:

- poor inter-personal skills
- basic hygiene problems
- lack of confidence
- gaps in their knowledge of the curriculum

## The Royal Manchester Children's Hospital School: an alternative educational setting for pupils with health and medical needs

*By J. G. Ashley*

The RMCHS provides an all-age facility within Salford, for children and young people who experience short-, medium- and long-term health or medically related conditions. The provision is as follows:

- Ward teaching and support for patients across the North West region and occasionally beyond (treating conditions such as childhood cancers, head injuries, renal failure, surgical needs).

- A Day School for up to 45 full- and part-time pupils (aged 11–16) referred to us by the Child and Adolescent Mental Health Service (CAMHS) due to their mental health needs (e.g. phobias, clinical depression, trauma).
- A Psychiatric Day Unit where school staff work alongside the CAMHS team in assessing pupils (aged 5–14) with possible mental health needs.
- 16–19 education and support at the Hope Hospital (now Salford Royal) for young people who have been hospitalized.
- Hospital support (home tuition) for Salford pupils who are either recovering or who are unable to attend school due health or medically related needs.
- A developing outreach support service to assist mainstream schools in the identification and support of vulnerable pupils in primary and secondary settings.

Staff members at RMCH are very experienced and knowledgeable, not only in regard to their teaching and support specialisms, but in specific aspects of SEN, counselling and holistic approaches. Pupil outcomes in the Day School are very good in regard to baselines on admission (e.g. numbers of pupils gaining A*–C in their GCSEs). We have developed an Every Child Matters profiling system that enables staff to work with pupils and their parents to determine strengths and areas for development in regard to ECM criteria. Such work has enabled effective holistic assessment and intervention in support of vulnerable children and young people. We have shared this approach with a local high school and have recorded some excellent outcomes in regard to reducing absence and exclusion rates while impacting positively upon pupils' academic achievements, attitudes and behaviour.

For further information about RMCH, please visit our website at: www.rmch.salford.sch.uk

*J. G. Ashley is the Headteacher of the RMCH*

# Improving alternative educational provision

In order to be effective, alternative education should include all the requirements that are necessary for successful youth development (see Smith and Thomas 2001 in Aron 2003). These requirements include:

- providing physically and psychologically safe facilities
- having a clear organization, well-defined goals and rules
- providing supportive relationships with adults and peers
- promoting positive behaviours
- being student-centred
- promoting autonomy and providing an empowering and challenging experience
- providing a sense of community
- integrating family, school and the community
- having well-trained, supportive teachers and a good pupil-teacher ratio
- being inclusive and addressing individual needs
- providing post-programme support

While many alternative education initiatives do provide excellent facilities and opportunities for such vulnerable children, few meet all the requirements listed above, and both research findings and Ofsted reports have highlighted a number of concerns. These concerns, according to Kendall et al. (2003), include:

- the 'paucity' of relevant information provided about each pupil on referral
- a shortage of skilled staff and a lack of time to deal with children's very specific, complex emotional and behavioural needs
- significant levels of non-attendance
- the 'continued vulnerability' of some pupils who remain engaged in criminal offences
- lack of resources

## Summary

In the past, pupils who were excluded from school, had committed crimes or had long-term illness, were often viewed as 'problem children'. Their needs were often ignored and they could easily become 'invisible' within the system. Education provided by so-called 'alternative educational contexts' was often seen as a sort of Cinderella service, and as we said before, a dumping ground for problem youth. However, there is now a general recognition that there is a need to improve the educational attainment of all pupils, and the DCSF has therefore given a commitment to improving the quality of current alternative provision. Recently, a White Paper: 'Back on track: A strategy for modernising alternative provision for young people' has been launched.

> This Paper sets out the Government's proposals for transforming alternative provision into a vibrant and successful part of the whole education system, working in close partnership with mainstream schools, special schools and with children's services, to meet the needs of all individual young people and set them back on the path to success. (DCSF 2008)

Thus, there will be a thrust towards providing more innovative alternatives to current provision, which could, for example, include more e-learning and virtual provision for some children (DCSF 2008).

### Key references

Klein, R. (2000), *Defying Disaffection: How Schools Are Winning the Hearts and Minds of Reluctant Students* (second edition). Stoke on Trent: Trentham.

## Useful websites

www.yjb.gov.uk
   The Youth Justice Board
www.Prus.org.uk
   National Organisation for Pupil Referral Units

# Part Five
## Education Revisited

# Education in the Future  **11**

## Future Studies

*Tomorrow's world will be shaped by our children's vision of it. What kind of vision will it be, and how can education help to shape it? These questions raise two sets of issues. One has to do with the contribution that education must make to society; the other relates to the expansion and reform of the education system itself so that it can meet the hopes and expectations that society has vested in it.*

*(Mayor 1997: 40)*

According to Power (2006) the course of education is dependent on the kind of society in which we wish to live in the future. While global issues are of importance, it is the types of policies and initiatives that are adopted that actually shape the nature of any future education system. So how do we decide on the future direction that education and also other social institutions should take? Increasingly, governments and businesses use so-called *Future Studies* as a means of anticipating future wants, needs and trends in their strategic planning. The idea that you can predict, or forecast, what the future holds is, of course, not new. In the 1960s, however, the new discipline of Future Studies arose as a means of applying a more academic approach to predicting the future implications of the then emerging technologies. Since then, the discipline has grown to consider what Sandford and

Facer term the 'possible, probable and preferable futures' of a variety of social institutions (2008: 5).

## Approaches to Future Studies

Future Studies employs a number of tried and tested social science methodologies, including surveys, questionnaires and focus groups, to collect, in the main, qualitative data which is then used to inform prediction and forecasting. According to Sandford and Facer (2008: 5), such methods are used either to:

- provide accounts of the past and the present in order to establish a context for future developments; *or:*
- provide an insight, both from experts and the general public, into people's attitudes and beliefs about the future

The information gained can be used in a variety of ways to build future visions and possibilities. It should be noted, however, that such predictions can be extremely unreliable (Ridgeway 2008). For example, in the 1970s it was considered that in the future only three computers would be needed worldwide! (Daanen and Facer 2007: 5). It is also important to note that, although some future studies involve a systematic analysis of the findings on which predictions are based, others involve more unfettered 'blue sky thinking' and are therefore less grounded in the evidence. Most predictions and forecasts also tend to reflect the needs and concerns of the people who have constructed them (Sandford and Facer 2008: 6).

Two of the most widely used methods in Future Studies are the Delphi Method and the use of scenarios, both relying heavily on the input of experts in order to contextualise trends:

**The Delphi Method** was devised in 1953 by the Rand Corporation to predict the future consequences of new technologies. It involves the use of rounds of questionnaires and controlled feedback that are used to elicit the views of a panel of experts, which then inform the future predictions.

**Scenarios** form the basis of many Future Studies. They are basically 'stories about the future' (Sandford and Facer 2008: 6), which enable people to test assumptions about the outcomes of present actions. Scenario building involves the monitoring of current trends in order to inform decisions about the future impact of proposals. It also involves the use of modelling and simulation in order to compare how relationships between the different variables play out in the different scenarios.

Daanen and Facer (2007) suggest that there has been a 'rash of crystal ball gazing' in the UK and also in other countries. Organizations like the UN and the OECD have also engaged in exploring possible futures for education in the twenty-first century. In the UK, such Future Studies include:

- 2020 Vision – the report of the Teaching and Learning in 2020 Review Group, considering approaches to personalized learning.

- The Building Schools for the Future Programme – looking at the kinds of institutions and structures that will be needed in the next 50 years.
- The QCA 21st-Century Curriculum Review, which considered the aims, purposes and nature of education in the UK over the next 100 years, which informed the 'Big Picture' and the 'Curriculum for the Future'.
- Beyond Current Horizons, a DCSF initiative with Futurelab, which is currently considering the long-term impacts of socio-technological change on education to 2025 and beyond.

# Future challenges

By the year 2050, the population of the world will be larger, older, more urban and also growing more slowly (Cohen 2007 in Schoetzau 2007). We will also have to cope with the consequences of the HIV/AIDS pandemic particularly in Africa, and the after effects of September 11 and of various conflicts worldwide. Other challenges include increasing globalization, the advancement of new technologies, the impact of migration, the emergence of alternative education methods and preparing individuals for jobs that have not yet been invented (see Sanborn et al. 2005). As Mayor (1997) suggests, although these are universal challenges, the solutions to those challenges are of necessity going to be local.

While these challenges will obviously influence future choices for education, Power (2006) suggests that there are nine strategic directions that can be followed when developing future education provision to help alleviate some of these issues. These are:

- strengthening public education
- developing learning throughout life
- providing a basic education for all children
- expanding and diversifying post-primary education
- improving the quality of education for all
- improving the status and quality of teaching
- integrating appropriate technologies
- educating for responsible citizenship
- educating for sustainable development

Mayor (1997), too, points to further influences on the direction that education should take, suggesting that education in the future should promote peace, democracy and human rights. He also suggests that particular attention should be paid to the education of women because of the positive effects that can accrue from this.

In the past, the nations that have prospered have been those that have invested heavily in education and training for all members of their societies. Their systems have been open systems that, according to Power, have 'encouraged critical reflection and debate, innovation, research and problem solving' (2006: 173). Power also suggests that:

> The real challenge is to do things differently in our governments, schools, colleges and universities. We need to think beyond the short-term and the expedient. We need to think globally. We need'

to act locally. We need to invest in educating for tomorrow. We need to renew our commitment to equity and fair play. We need to insist on quality. We need to educate for global citizenship and sustainable development. We need to ensure that governments are held accountable for meeting their educational obligations, and keep their promises. To do so, we need to work together, that is, to build a strong local and regional education community supporting the efforts of local and multilateral organisations committed to improving the quality of education for all. (Power 2006: 173)

# Future possibilities

Before we look at a few of the possible future scenarios for education that have been proposed, it is worth pausing to consider some of the things that could inform those scenarios, for example the types of new technologies that might be available, the kinds of alternative learning systems that could feasibly be put in place and also the kind of learners we might need in the future.

## New technologies

> Education will not be changed simply as a result of a given invention or discovery, but by the ways in which these developments are incorporated into social life (changing our values and goals for education) or into educational practice (changing the methods and tools we have available to education).
>
> (Sandford and Facer 2008: 3)

The past thirty years have seen an unsurpassed growth in new technologies and in their socioeconomic importance, particularly with the emergence of the personal computer and the internet. However, such advances may be overshadowed by the impact of some of the new emerging technologies, particularly the post-genomic biotechnologies of 'protomics' and 'synthetic life' (Cliff et al. 2008: 1). The following are examples of just some of the technological developments that may have a significant impact on education in the future.

### Ubiquitous computing – the 'internet of things'

We are already very used to the ubiquitous nature of mobile phones, GPS technology and wireless broadband internet access. It is possible that the use of digital technologies will become even more widespread and that by 2030 'every physical object that we use, consume, interact with, walk through or around will be logged continuously via what is called the "internet of things"'(Cliff et al. 2008: 4). Daanen and Facer (2007: 10) suggest that life will, therefore, become increasingly technologically enhanced and that we may have to reconceptualize concepts such as intelligence and thinking to accommodate the way in which we use and interact with such technologies. They also suggest that the ubiquitous use of technology may have profound implications for education, particularly with respect to equity of access to such resources and also with respect to assessment (ibid.) – consider the resistance to the use of calculators in maths tests and examinations.

## Intelligent environments

A facet of the notion of ubiquitous computing is the concept of intelligent environments. With digital technologies and tiny sensors or 'motes' embedded into everything around you, the environment can become responsive and adaptive to an individual's needs. It is possible, therefore, that in the future, schools will find it easier to provide a so-called 'built pedagogy' that will provide an educational environment that is more flexible, responsive and more easily personalized to suit an individual's needs (Daanen and Facer 2007: 5).

## Brain-world interfaces and cognitive enhancement

Creating *direct interfaces* between neurons in the brain and computer devices holds significant potential. We can already see successful examples of such technologies in the form of cochlear implants to restore hearing, and heart pacemakers. It seems possible that such devices could be used to replace damaged limbs and also to help older people overcome the effects of aging (Cliff et al. 2008). There is also the future possibility of making direct interfaces with specific parts of the brain (Daanen and Facer 2007). However, such technologies also present what Cliff et al. (2008: 7) suggest is the rather Orwellian spectre of implanting devices such as Radio Frequency Identification chips into people, as they currently do with pet dogs and cats. The use of GPS tracking devices, for example, is already being used by researchers in order to envisage how young people use urban spaces, although it is very easy to conceive of more sinister uses of such technology.

The facility to *enhance cognitive ability* is already a possibility. Smart drugs or 'cogs' are currently used in medicine to enhance memory or attention span. Although they have been designed to help people with ADHD and Alzheimer's disease, they are increasingly being used by healthy people. Cliff et al. (2008: 5) point to an article in *Nature* that suggested that one in five of its readers had participated in 'brain-doping', taking drugs like Ritalin and Inderal as a means of improving their memory in order to pass examinations or to improve their performance at work. This raises real issues for educators, similar to those experienced in sport, where individuals who use performance enhancing drugs are viewed as 'drugs cheats'. If cognitive enhancing substances are not banned, one can imagine some parents electing for their children to use them in order to do well in their examination and thus possibly helping to eradicate the effects of natural biological differences in ability (ibid.).

There are also a number of *other technologies* such as Artificial Intelligence, 3D printing, the 'Semantic Internet' and the 'Pragmatic Internet' (developed to aid more intelligent searches on the web) that also have the potential to influence education. However, as Ridgeway (2008) points out, we should be cautious about our ability to predict the future and, in particular, to predict the future impact of any one technology. As he points out, current ICT initiatives have had little effect, either on what goes on in classrooms or on children's achievement. He also points to a further challenge presented by such new technologies, that of finding teachers with the necessary training and skills to use them effectively.

## Types of learning systems

*When mass schooling was established, people lived in an information-poor environment. Assembling large numbers of children together in one place called a school, with teachers who had been exposed to the scarce information, made a kind of sense . . . For education in the future there are three basic options. One is to retain the present schooling system, a second is to modify the existing system and a third is to develop a completely new system.*

*(Meighan and Harber 2007: 447, 448)*

The question for the future of education is that, although schools may have made sense in the past, will they continue to make sense? As Meyer (2007) points out, the current way in which schools are organized, with same age groupings, a 9 a.m. – 4 p.m. school day and long summer holidays, does not sit well with modern lifestyles and with the ways in which we can utilize new technological developments. However, rather than abandoning schools altogether, we need to reconceptualize how schools are organized and function so that they can best serve our future needs and wants.

### Flexischooling

The notion of flexischooling, originated by Holt and Meighan in 1984, is based on the idea that 'rigid systems produce rigid people, flexible systems produce flexible people' (Meighan and Harber 2007: 471). In this vision of an alternative learning system, school, home and family are viewed as a partnership. According to Meighan and Harber (2007), many of the components of flexischooling, what they term the *learning resources centres* are already available, it is the operational mechanisms that need to be addressed. They present the main rationale of flexischooling (ibid.) as being that:

- education does not have a single location – there can be several linked learning resources centres including the home, school, museums, etc.
- parents and carers take a more active role in their child's education
- new relationships are established between the learner and the teacher, learning does not always have to be directly facilitated by the teacher
- home resources, such as TV and computers, can be utilized
- individual differences are respected and accommodated

There are obviously issues associated with such an approach. As Valentine suggests, in trying to redefine the relationship between what she terms 'the spaces of home, school and community', we have to be aware of the potential pitfalls (2008: 1). First, there is the issue of the blurring of the boundaries between home, school, work and leisure, i.e. between the public and the private space. This, Valentine (2008) suggests, may lead to children redefining their leisure and play activities, like watching TV or playing on their computer, as school activities with the result that they may be less keen to pursue them. Valentine also points to the fact that there are considerable variations in children's home environments, particularly with respect to the child's ability to access technology, and also the ability or desire of parents/carers to support their children's learning. Such differences will obviously lead to inequalities in a system that is based on an equality of provision for all, thus raising the question of how such disadvantage could be overcome (ibid.).

## The extended school

*Open twenty-four hours a day. Different kids arrive at different times. They don't all come at the same time, like an army. They don't just ring the bells at the same time. They're different kids. They have different potentials . . . I would be running a twenty–four hour school. I would have non-teachers working with teachers in that school, I would have the kids coming and going at different times that make sense for them. We're individualizing time; we're personalizing time. We're not having everyone arrive at the same time, leave at the same time . . . schools have to be completely integrated into the community, to take advantage of the skills in the community.*

*(Alvin Toffler at www.eutopia.org/future-school in Valentine 2008: 1)*

In the future, schools could be expected to provide much wider community access. According to Valentine (2008), this could include the concept of the 24 hour school, enabling learners to choose when they want to learn, extended community and business use incorporated into the site and the creation of open learning centres such as cyber cafes and crèches. As Valentine suggests, this will not only involve redesigning schools with a more integrated use of ICT, but will involve teachers, learners and society as a whole reconceptualizing the concept of the school. Valentine also points out that such radical changes in the way schools function raises the issue of how children will be supervised when their parents and carers are working, and how such changes will impact on the world of work.

## New sites for learning

The advent of ICT and the rapid developments in so-called 'e-learning' have led to the concept of 'online learning sites'. According to Valentine, such sites provide a new kind of learning community where children can engage with other children in different parts of the country or even the world, can explore virtual museums and art galleries and even interact with astronauts on the space station. The extensive use of online learning, she suggests, raises the issue of how we manage these new 'information landscapes' and provide pupils with the new skills they need in order to identify reliable sources and avoid plagiarism (2008: 5).

In the future, it is expected that as well as increasing the use of online learning, pupils will increasingly engage in a range of learning outside the classroom, in so called off-line learning. Increasingly formal learning will come to encompass the use of the home, museums, libraries and other situations that have previously been associated with leisure activities and more informal learning (ibid.).

## Virtual schools

The extension of the use of online, e-learning is the notion of virtual schools or universities. Many such institutions are now starting to emerge, although some, like NotSchool and the Open University, are already well established. NotSchool, for example, is a virtual learning space designed for children of school age who are unable to cope with mainstream provision. It provides the learners, or researchers as they are termed, with access to tuition aimed at gaining traditional qualifications. The learners are supported by online tutors and mentors (for more information visit www.notschool.net). The Open University is an extremely successful example of adult distance learning using a wide variety of information communication technologies (Rix and Twining 2007; Meighan and Harber 2007).

According to Harrison (2006), Glen Russell from Monash University predicts the following three forms of Virtual Schools in the future:

**Independent schools** where both the time of access and the learning are personalized to the students' needs and wants.

**Synchronous schools** where students engage in a schedule of learning activities in concert with other students and teachers through the use of online discussions and video-conferencing.

**Broadcast schools** where students are simply able to access the school's resources on the web.

One of the main issues raised by the notion of the virtual school is the fact that children 'attending' such schools will lack the face-to-face interactions and socialization that traditional schooling provides, a concern that in the past has been levelled at homeschooling.

Virtual schools are also being used in other ways. For example, the National College for School Leadership, the BBC and the Centre for Educational Leadership in Manchester have, together, developed a virtual school where teachers and school leaders can act out expert-developed, scenario-based simulations within a computer-generated school environment in order to see the consequences and possible alternative approaches to certain situations (for more information visit http://devvirtualschool.ncsl.org.uk/).

### Activity 11.1

Visit Microsoft's website at www.microsoft.com/Education/SchoolofFutureVision and explore its resources on the British government's 'Building Schools for the Future Programme' (2003). The site also allows you to explore Microsoft's vision of 'Connected Learning Communities' and view case studies of successful 'Schools for the Future' projects.

## Types of learners

Schools generally tend to teach people to be smart rather than wise. Sternberg (2004) suggests, however, that there are several reasons why we should strive for wisdom to be taught.

He suggests that developing wisdom, rather than just knowledge, is more likely to promote happiness and satisfaction, develop value judgements, provide a way to creating greater harmony and provide more just parents and citizens. According to Sternberg:

> At some level, we as a society have a choice. What do we wish to maximize through our schooling? Is it just knowledge? Is it just intelligence? Or is it also wisdom? If it is wisdom, then we need to put our students on a much different course. We need to value not only how they use their outstanding individual abilities to maximize their attainments but how they use their individual abilities to maximize the attainment of others as well. We need in short, to value wisdom. And then we need to remember that wisdom is not just about what we think, but more importantly how we act. (Sternberg 2004: 76)

---

### Activity 11.2

Reflect on the views presented in Chapter 2 concerning notions about what it means to be educated. How well does Sternberg's vision of a future learner ideal of someone who is both 'wise and smart' fit with the characteristics of Burbules' vision of the educated person of the future?

---

# Future scenarios

According to Newby, 'To construct a scenario is to imagine a state of affairs, which might, one day, come true . . . (however,) the unknown future must grow out of the known present if it is to make any sense at all' (2005: 255). A number of future scenarios have been constructed for education. Newby presents three such scenarios, originally developed by the OECD as part of their work on future schools, 'brief think pieces' designed to promote discussion and debate (2005: 254). The scenarios presented by Newby are summarized below.

### Education everywhere

In this vision of the future, schools, and also teachers as we know them today, no longer exist and education has been deinstitutionalized. State schools only exist as a catch-net for an educational underclass who do not have access to the 'digital economy'. Education is, literally, everywhere, networked, for example through homes, churches, sports and community centres. Homeschooling is commonplace. In this networked society, flexibility, individualism and non-formalized learning are the recipe of the day. Education is delivered both online and off-line, through networks of parents, learners and a variety of professionals, including educators.

### Gifts, actually

This future vision presents a society in which a focus on personal enterprise and individualism has led to a breakdown in social cohesion. Schools, as a consequence, have become the locus of a counter-revolution, providing a focus for community collaboration and shared identity. This vision sits well with the concept of the 'extended school', open 24/7 and acting as the hub, providing a range of services, not all educational, to all members of the community. In this future, the main purpose of the school is not education – that is readily available online – schools focus more on personal and social development.

### The education marketplace

In the final vision, education has succumbed to market forces. Total deregulation of the system has led to the 'consumer' being king and choice the buzzword. Education is increasingly individualized with tailor-made programmes. Business sponsorship of education has grown, with large multinationals producing not only educational software but accrediting qualifications, thus having considerable power over what people learn. Learning has become a commodity. Schools focus on learning how to learn, and teachers have to be experts in the application of new technologies and software. Schools are big business.

While such scenarios are interesting to consider, it is difficult to predict which direction education will take in the future. What emerges from such deliberations is, however, a sense of a number of common themes that will influence in some way what education looks like in the future (see also Newby 2005: 260). These include:

- the extent to which new technologies are used and incorporated into educational practice
- the way in which people interact with schools and their local communities – will individualism or collaboration prevail?
- the way in which public and private spaces are conceived
- the level of central and local government control

What none of the scenarios considered, was the cost of such changes and also the role of tradition. In England, we have inherited both a physical infrastructure and an educational tradition that is deeply rooted in the nation's psyche. How far the rise of new technology and more flexible ways of living will help to alter our views about what schools are for, remains a big question. Similarly, none of the future visions are possible without significant financial inputs from the government and/or business. It is therefore possible that the school of 2050 will very closely resemble that of today.

---

### Activity 11.3

What is your vision of education in the year 2020 and, looking even further ahead, in the year 2050? There are a number of questions that inform most future predictions about education (source www.beyondcurrenthorizons.org.uk and www.futurelab.org.uk) that you can use to form your response, such as:

- What will the aims and purposes of education be?
- What will education institutions look like?
- How will education be organized, governed, etc.?
- Who will be involved and what will their roles be?
- How will learning be supported?
- Should children be made to resist or rely on technology?
- Where do schools need to be, where does learning need to take place?
- How will equity and fairness be assured?

# Summary

We leave you, at the end of our journey and yours, with the words of Federico Mayor, who as Director General of UNESCO in 1997 suggested that it was:

> Our duty as educators is to use education to focus the energy and idealism of young people on building a society of peace, progress and prosperity. We must strengthen the function of peace-building in all cultures. We must infuse into the minds of young people everywhere a new ethic of sharing and caring. We must prepare the ground for a new civilization in which the word and not the sword prevail. (Mayor 1997: 41)

## Key references

DfES (2003), *Building Schools for the Future*. London: DfES.

DfES (2006), *2020 Vision: The Report of the Teaching and Learning in 2020 Review Group*. Nottingham: DfES.

Meighan, R. and Harber, C. (2007), *A Sociology of Educating*. London: Continuum.

## Useful websites

www.beyondcurrenthorizons.org.uk
> The Beyond Current Horizons website: a DCSF initiative with Futurelab, considering the long-term impacts of socio-technological change on education to 2025 and beyond

www.futurelab.org.uk
> The website of Futurelab, involved in research and innovation in the use of digital and other technologies

www.qca.org.uk/qca_6073.aspx
> The QCA Futures – a national conversation about the future of learning in the UK

www.microsoft.com/Education/SchoolofFutureVision.mspx
> Part of Microsoft's education website concerned with Building Schools for the Future

# References

Apple, M. W. (2001), *Educating the 'Right' Way*. London: Routledge Falmer.

Apple, M. W. (2004), *Ideology and Curriculum* (third edition). London: Routledge Falmer.

Apple, M. W. (2007), 'Who needs teacher education? Gender, technology, and the work of home schooling', *Teacher Education Quarterly*, 34, 2, 111.

Arnove, R. F. (2007), 'Introduction: Reframing comparative education: The dialectic of the global and the local' in Arnove, R. F. and Torres, C. A. (eds) *Comparative Education: The Dialectic of the Global and the Local* (third edition). Lanham: Rowman & Littlefield.

Aron, L. Y. (2003), *Towards a Typology of Educational Programs: A Compilation of Elements from the Literature*. Washington: The Urban Institute.

Arnot, D. M. and Weiner, G. (1999), *Closing the Gender Gap: Post-war Education and Social Change*. Cambridge: Polity Press.

Athey, C. (1994), *Extending Thought in Young Children: A Parent-Teacher Partnership*. London: Paul Chapman Publishing.

Avenarius, H. and Liket, T. M. E. (2000), 'Systems of public administration: Patterns of school legislation and management' in Swing, E. S., Schriever, J. and Orivel, F. (eds) *Problems and Perspectives in European Education*. West Port, CT: Prager.

Baker, M. (2004), 'What is the point of a specialist future?', *Times Educational Supplement*, 4385, 22.

Balls, E. (2008), 'How the government is supporting the 21st century school', *Education Guardian.Co.Uk*, 3 July 2008, *http://education.guardian.co.uk/schools/comment/story/0,2288807,00.html* (accessed 24 July 2008).

Ballantine, J. H. and Spade, J. Z. (eds) (2008), *Schools and Society: A Sociological Approach to Education* (third edition). Los Angeles: Pine Forge Press.

Barrow, R. (1999), 'The importance of aims in education' in Marples, R. *The Aims of Education*. London: Routledge.

Barrow, R. and Woods, R. (2006), *An Introduction to the Philosophy of Education* (fourth edition). Oxford: Routledge.

Bartlett, S., Burton, D. and Peim, N. (2001), *Introduction to Education Studies*. London: Paul Chapman.

Bartlett, S. and Burton, D. (2007). *Introduction to Education Studies* (second edition). London: Sage.

Bekerman, Z., Burbules, N. C. and Silberman-Keller, D. (eds) (2006, 2007) *Learning in Places: The Informal Education Reader*. New York: Peter Lang.

Benavot, A. (2006), 'The Diversification of Secondary Education: School Curricula in Comparative Perspective', IBE Working Papers on Curriculum Issues No 6. Available at: *www.ibe.unesco.org* (accessed 2 August 2008).

BBC (2001), 'Comprehensive ideal "not dead"', Tuesday 13 February 2001, 17:12 GMT. Available at: *http://news.bbc.co.uk/1/hi/education/1167835.stm* (accessed 28 July 2008).

Blair, M., Holland, J. and Sheldon, S. (eds) (1995), *Identity and Diversity: Gender and the Experience of Education: A Reader*. Berkshire: OUP.

Boden, M. (1994), *Piaget* (second edition). London: Fontana.

Bourdieu, P. (2004), 'The forms of capital' in Ball, S. J. (ed.) *The Routledge Falmer Reader in Sociology of Education*. Abingdon: Routledge Falmer.

Bowles, S. and Gintis, H. (1976), *Schooling in Capitalist America*. London: Routledge and Kegan Paul.

Braggins, J. and Talbot, J. (2005), *Wings of Learning: The Role of the Prison Officer in Supporting Prisoner Education*. The Centre for Crime and Justice Studies.

Branigan, T. (2002), 'Top school's creationists preach value of Biblical story over evolution: State funded secondary teachers do not accept the findings of Darwin', *The Guardian* March 9 2002. Available at: *www.guardian.co.uk/uk/2002/mar/09/schools.religion* (accessed 2 August 2008).

Brighouse, T. (2007), *Accidents Can Happen. www.qca.org.uk/qca_6128.aspx* (accessed 5 August 2008).

Brisard, E. and Menter, I. (2008), 'Compulsory education in the United Kingdom' in Matheson, D. (ed.) *An Introduction to the Study of Education* (third edition). Oxford: Routledge.

Brown, C. S. (1988), *Like it Was: A Complete Guide to Writing Oral History*. New York: Teachers & Writers Collaborative.

Brunner, D. D. (1994), *Inquiry and Reflection: Framing Narrative Practice in Education*. New York: Suny Press.

Burbules, N. C. (2002), 'Where is philosophy of education today: At the start of a new millennium, or at the end of a tired old one?', *Philosophical Studies in Education*, 33, 13–23.

Burke, B. (2000), 'Post-modernism and post-modernity', *The Encyclopaedia of Informal Education, www.infed.org/biblio/b.postmd.htm* (accessed 29 August 2008).

Chitty, C. (2002), *Understanding Schools and Society*. London: Routledge.

Chrispeels, J. H. (1992), *Purposeful Restructuring: Creating a Culture for Learning and Achievement in Elementary Schools*. London: The Falmer Press.

Cliff, D., O'Malley, C. and Taylor, J. (2008), 'Future issues in socio-technological change for UK education', *www.beyondcurrenthorizons.org.uk* (accessed 2 August 2008).

Coelen, T. (2003), '"Full-time" education systems in the knowledge society: International comparisons of the co-operation between schools and out-of-school agencies'. Paper presented at the European Conference on Educational Research. University of Hamburg, 17–20 September 2003. Available from Education online at *www.leeds.ac.uk/educol/documents/00003521.html* (accessed 17 June 2008).

Colclough, C. (2005), 'Policy arena: Rights, goals and targets: How do those for education add up?', *Journal of International Development*, 17, 101–111.

Colley, H., Hodkinson, P. and Malcolm, J. (2002), *Non-Formal Learning: Mapping the Conceptual Terrain: A Consultation Report*. Leeds: University of Leeds Lifelong Learning Institute. Also available in the *informal education archives* at *www.infed.org/archives/e-texts/colley_informal_learning.htm* (accessed 8 August 2008).

Connell, J. H. (1980), 'Diversity and the coevolution of competitors or the ghost of competition past', *Oikos*, 35, 2, 131–138.

Cooney, W., Cross, C. and Trunk, B. (1993), *From Plato To Piaget*. Maryland: University Press of America, Inc.

Corner, T. and Grant, N. (2008), 'Comparing education systems' in Matheson, D. (ed.) *An Introduction to the Study of Education* (third edition). Oxford: Routledge.

Corrigan, M. and Chapman, P. (2008), 'Trust in teachers: A motivating element to learning', *Radical Pedagogy*, 9.

Crossley, M. and Watson, K. (2003), *Comparative and International Research in Education. Globalization, Context and Difference*. London: Taylor and Francis.

Csikszentmihalyi, M. (1990), *Flow: The Psychology of Optimal Experience*. New York: Harper and Row.

Curtis, C. A. (1998), 'Cultural reflections: The use of autobiography in the teacher education classroom', *Education*, Fall, 28.

Davies, I., Gregory, I. and McGuinn, N. (2002), *Key Debates in Education*. London: Continuum.

Daanen, H. and Facer, K. (2007), '2020 and Beyond: Future Scenarios for Education in the Age of New Technologies', *www.futurelab.org.uk/openingeducation* (accessed 2 August 2008).

Darder, A. (1995), 'Buscando America: The contributions of critical Latino educators to the academic development and empowerment of Latino students in the US' in Sleeter, C. and McLaren, P. *Multicultural Education, Critical Pedagogy and the Politics of Difference*. New York: Suny Press.

Department for Children Schools and Families (2004), *Every Child matters*, *www.everychildmatters.gov.uk* (accessed 1 September 2008).

Department for Children Schools and Families (2007), *Faith in the System*. Nottingham: DCSF Publications. Available at: *www.dcsf.gov.uk/publications/faithinthesystem/pdfs/FaithInTheSystem.pdf* (accessed 8 September 2008).

Department for Children Schools and Families (2008), *Statutory Framework for the Early Years Foundation Stage: Setting the Standards for Learning, Development and Care of Children Aged Birth to Five*. London: HMSO.

Department for Education and Science (1989), *National Curriculum: from Policy to Practice*. London: DES.

Department for Education and Employment/Qualifications and Curriculum Authority (1999), *National Curriculum Handbook for Teachers in England*. London: HMSO.

Department for Education and Employment (2001), *Opportunity for All in a World of Change: A White Paper on Enterprise, Skills and Innovation*. Norwich: Stationary Office.

Department for Education and Skills (2002), 'Extending opportunity: Raising standards', *www.dfes.gov.uk/14-19greenpaper/download/raisingstandards.pdf* (accessed 17 June 2008).

Department for Education and Skills (2002a), *Extended Schools: Providing Opportunities and Services for All*. London: DfES.

Department for Education and Skills (2003), *Building Schools for the Future*. London: DfES.

Department for Education and Skills and TNS Social Research (2003), 'Survey of alternative provision', *www.dcsf.gov.uk/behaviourandattendance/about/newsdetails* (accessed 3 September 2008).

Department for Education and Skills and the Office for Standards in Education (2004), *A New Relationship with Schools*. London: DES.

Department for Education and Skills and the Office for Standards in Education (2005), *Extended Schools: Access to Opportunities and Services for All: A Prospectus*. London: DfES. Available at *www.teachernet.gov.uk/extendedschools* (accessed 10 September 2008).

Devine, N. (2007), 'Prison education in a modern context'. Paper presented at BERA, 5–8 September 2007.

Directgov (2008), 'Access to education for children and young people with medical needs', *www.direct.gov.uk/en/Parents/Schoolslearninganddevelopment* (accessed 11 August 2008).

Driver, S. and Martell, L. (2006), *New Labour*. London: Polity.

Education Otherwise Website, *www.education_otherwise.org*

Edwards, T. (2002), 'Restructuring educational opportunity in England', *Australian Journal of Education*, 46, 2, 109–120.

Edwardians Online Website, *www.qualidata.ac.uk/edwardians*

Eurydice (2007–8), 'The education system of England, Wales and Northern Ireland 2007/8', The Information Database on Education Systems in Europe, *www.eurydice.org.uk* (accessed 22 June 2008).

Evans, J. (2007), 'Macs prove essential for excluded pupils', *www.macworld.com* (accessed 6 August 2008).

Early Years Foundation Stage (2008), *www.standards.dfes.gov.uk/eyfs*

Fishman, S. M. and McCarthy, L. (1998), *John Dewey and the Challenge of Classroom Practice*. New York: Teachers College Press.

Freeman, M. (2000), 'The future of children's rights', *Children and Society*, 14, 227–293.

Garratt, D. and Pickard, A. (2007), 'Tales of reflexive learning: Knowing less and seeking more in student experience'. (Unpublished) Manchester Metropolitan University.

Gartner, A., Latham, G. and Merritt, S. (1996), 'The power of narrative: Transcending disciplines', Original ultiBASE publication, *http://ultibase.rmit.edu.au/Articles/dec96/gartn1.htm* (accessed 25 August 2008).

Gefter, A. (2006), 'Preach your children well: Special report: Home-schooling', *New Scientist*, 1922577 (11 November), 20–24.

Gillborn, D. and Youdell, D. (2000), *Rationing Education*. London: Routledge.

Gilroy, P. (1999), 'The aims of education and the philosophy of education: The pathology of an argument' in Marples, R. *The Aims of Education*. London: Routledge.

Green, A. (1990), *Education and State Formation: The Rise of Education Systems in England, France and the USA*. Basingstoke: Macmillan Press.

Greenaway, E. (1999), 'Lower secondary education: An international comparison', *www.inca.org.uk.pdflower_secondary_no_intro_99.pdf* (accessed 29 July 2008).

Gregory, I. (2002), 'The aims of education' in Davies, I., Gregory, I. and McGuinn, N. *Key Debates in Education*. London: Continuum.

Grek, S. (2004), 'Whose story do museums tell? Researching museums as sites of adult learning'. Paper presented at SCUTREA 34th Annual Conference, University of Sheffield, 6–8 July 2004.

Grek, S. (2005), 'Critical ethnography and museum education: The pursuit of in-depth analysis of visitor learning experiences'. Paper presented at the European Conference on Educational Research, University College Dublin, 7–10 September 2005.

Grinter, R. (2000), 'Single issues to coherent campaign: Pitfalls and possibilities' in Shah, S. *Equality Issues for the New Millennium*. Aldershot: Ashgate.

Hanley, M. S. (2006), 'Education: Transmission and transformation', *Journal of Thought*, Fall, 51–55.

Hammons, C. W. (2001), 'Home schooling', Education Next, *www.educationnext.org* (accessed 10 August 2008).

Harris, K. (1999), 'Aims! Whose Aims?' in Marples, R. *The Aims of Education*. London: Routledge.

Harris, N. (2005), 'Empowerment and state education: Rights of choice and participation', *The Modern Law Review*, 68, 6, 925–957.

Harrison, B. (2006), 'Virtually there? Building virtual schools for the future', Futurelab Web Articles, November 2006, *www.futurelab.org.uk/resources/publications_reports_articles/web_articles/Web_Article468* (accessed 20 August 2008).

Hargreaves, D. H. (1982), *The Challenge for the Comprehensive School: Culture, Curriculum and Community*. London: Routledge.

Hatcher, R. (2004), 'Social class and school' in Matheson, D. (ed.) *An Introduction to the Study of Education*. London: Routledge.

Heythrop Institute for Religion, Ethics and Public Life (2005), 'Faith schools', 4 November 2005, www. heythrop.ac.uk (accessed 2 August 2008).

HMSO (2004), 'The offenders' learning journey document', *http://offender-learning.qia.oxi.net/index.php?q=node/36* (accessed 10 August 2008).

ISC (2008), 'Independent schools Council census', *www.isc.co.uk* (accessed 10 September 2008).

Ikeda, D. (2001), *Soka Education: A Buddhist Vision for Teachers, Students and Parents*. Santa Monica: Middleway Press.

Inca (2007), 'Inca comparative tables: National educational aims', *www.inca.org.uk/pdf/table_3.pdf* (accessed 18 June 2008).

Inca (2008), 'International review of curriculum and assessment frameworks', *www.inca.org.uk* (accessed 23 May 2008).

Jackson, A. (2007), 'And some have communities thrust upon them: Prisons as learning communities'. Paper presented at the Standing Conference on University Teaching and Research in the Education of Adults, Belfast, July 2007.

Jackson, D. (1990), *Unmasking Masculinity: A Critical Autobiography*. London: Unwin.

James, N. (2005), '"Actup!" Theatre as education and its impact on young people's learning', *Working paper,* Centre for Labour Market Studies, University of Leicester. Available at: *www.clms.le.ac.uk/publications/workingpapers/working_paper46.pdf* (accessed 2 September 2008).

Jamieson, B. Z. (2008), 'Teach your children well: The first rule of any civilised society', *The Humanist*, 68.3 (May/June), 4–5.

Jones, L. M., Pickard, A. and Stronach, I. (2008), 'Primary schools: The professional environment', in *Primary Review Research Survey 6/2*. Cambridge: University of Cambridge Faculty of Education.

Jover, G. (2001), 'What does the right to education mean? A look at an international debate from legal, ethical and pedagogical points of view', *Studies in Philosophy and Education*, 20, 213–223.

Judge, H. (2002), 'Religion and the state: The case of faith-based schools', *The Political Quarterly*, 422–430.

Karpiak, I. (2000), 'Writing our life: Adult learning and teaching through autobiography', *Canadian Journal of University Continuing Education*, 26, 1, 31–50.

Kehily, M. J. (1995), 'Self narration, autobiography and identity construction', *Gender and Education*, 7, 1, 23–31.

Kellner, D. (2000), 'Multiple literacies and critical pedagogies' in Trifonas, P. P. (ed.) *Revolutionary Pedagogies: Cultural Politics, Instituting Education, and the Discourse of Theory*. London: Routledge.

Kendall, S., Kinder, K., Halsey, K., Fketcher-Morgan, C., White, R. and Brown, C. (2003), 'An evaluation of alternative education provision', NFER research brief, 403, March 2003.

Klein, R. (2000), *Defying Disaffection: How Schools are Winning the Hearts and Minds of Reluctant Students* (second edition). Stoke on Trent: Trentham.

Knowles, M. S. and associates (1984), *Andragogy in Action: Applying Modern Principles of Adult Education*. San Francisco: Jossey-Bass.

Koetzsch, R. E. (1997), *The Parents' Guide to Alternatives in Education*. Boston: Shambhala.

Kridel, C. (1998), *Writing Educational Biography: Explorations in Qualitative Research*. New York: Garland.

Lauder, H., Lowe, J. and Chawla-Duggan, R. (2008), 'Education: Changing Global Contexts' in *Primary Review Research Survey 1/4*. Cambridge: University of Cambridge Faculty of Education.

Laevers, F. (ed.) (1994), *Defining and Assessing Quality in Early Childhood Education*. Leuven: Studia Paedagogica, Leuven University Press.

Le Métais, J. (1997), 'Values and aims in curriculum and assessment frameworks', *www.inca.org.uk* (accessed 20 July 2008).

Le Métais, J. (2002), 'International developments in upper secondary education: Contexts, provision and issues', in NFER/QCA report for Inca: Thematic Study 8, *www.inca.org.uk/pdf/cav_final_report.pdf* (22 July 2008).

Levinson, B. A., Foley, D. E. and Holland, D. C. (1996), *The Cultural Production of the Educated Person: Critical Ethnographies of Schooling and Local Practice*. New York: Suny Press.

Lilley, I. (1967), *Friedrich Froebel: A Selection of His Writings*. Cambrigde: Cambridge University Press.

Lillard, P. P. (1972), *Montessori: A Modern Approach*. New York: Schocken Books.

Lohmann-Hancock, C. B. A. (2006), 'The influence of early practices of teaching and learning of basic skills to offenders: The impact of educational experiences on the choice and establishing a need to learn', paper presented at Bera, 6–9 September 2006.

Lord, P., Wilkin, A., Kinder, K., Murfield, J., Jones, M., Chamberlain, T., Easton, C., Martin, K., Gulliver, C., Paterson, C., Ries, J., Moor, H., Stott, A., Wilkin, C. and Stoney, S. (2006), *Analysis of Children and Young People's Plans 2006*. Slough: NFER.

Lynch, K. and O'Riorden, C. (1999), 'Inequality in higher education: A study of social class barriers' in Lynch, K. *Equality in Education*. Dublin: Gill and Macmillan.

Machin, S. and McNally, S. (2008), 'Aims for primary education: The changing national context' in *Primary Review Research Survey 1/3*. Cambridge: University of Cambridge Faculty of Education.

Marley, D. (2007), 'Faith Schools on the road to expansion', *Times Educational Supplement*, 14 September 2007.

Marples, R. (ed.) (1999), *The Aims of Education*. London: Routledge.

Marshall, J. D. (2006), 'The meaning of the concept of education: Searching for the lost arc', *Journal of Thought*. Fall, 33–37.

Martin, J. R. (1981), 'The ideal of the educated person', *Educational Theory*, 31, 2, 97–109.

Matheson, D. (ed.) (2008), *An Introduction to the Study of Education* (third edition). Oxford: Routledge.

Matheson, C. (2008), 'Ideology in education in the United Kingdom' in Matheson, D. (ed.) *An Introduction to the Study of Education* (third edition). Oxford: Routledge.

Maylor, U. (1995), 'Identity, migration and education' in Blair, M., Holland, J. and Sheldon, S. (eds) *Identity and Diversity: Gender and the Experience of Education: A Reader*. Berkshire: OUP.

Mayor, F. (1997), 'Education: The seedbed of the future', *The Unesco Courier*. January, 40–41.

Meighan, R. (1997), *The Next Learning System: And Why Home-schoolers are Trailblazers*. Nottingham: Educational Heretics Press.

Meighan, R. and Harber, C. (2007), *A Sociology of Educating*. London: Continuum.

Meyer, J. W., Ramirez, F. O. and Soysal, Y. N. (1992), 'World expansion of mass education: 1870–1980', *Sociology of Education*, 65, 2, 128–149.

Mitchell, C. et al. (eds) (2005), *Just Who Do We Think We Are? Methodologies for Autobiography and Self Study in Teaching*. London: Routledge Falmer.

Monteagudo, J. G. (2005), 'Educational autobiography in a university context: Our past and present through thought and feeling', paper presented to the Life History and Biography Network, Anghiari, Italy, 3–6 March 2005. Available at *http://esrea2005.ece.uth.gr/downloads* (accessed 22 August 2008).

Morgan-Klein, B. and Osborne, M. (2007), *The Concepts and Practices of Lifelong Learning*. London: Routledge.

Morrison, J. (2007), 'From Nice-but-dim to Loadsamoney: Changing media perceptions of the independent schools sector 1997–2006', report commissioned for the 2007 ISC Annual Conference by the Independent Schools Commission. Available at www.isc.co.uk (accessed 20 September 2008).

Myers, K. (2007), 'Do we still need schools?', *www.qca.org.uk/qca_6128.aspx* (accessed 5 August 2008).

National Statistics Online (2007), 'Society: Early years education: Two thirds of 3 and 4 year olds go to school', *www.statistics.gov.uk/cci/nugget_print.as p?ID=1766* (accessed 12 May 2008).

Neill, A. S. (1968), 'Summerhill' in Vaughan, M. (2006) (ed.) *Summerhill and A. S. Neill*. Maidenhead: OUP.

Newby, M. (2005), 'Looking to the future', *Journal of Education for Teaching*, 31, 4, 253–261.

Nieto, S. (1999), *The Light in Their Eyes: Creating Multicultural Learning Communities*. New York: Teachers College Press.

Noddings, N. (2007), *Philosophy of Education*. Colorado: Westview Press.

Novello, M. K. (1999), 'Jean-Jacques Rousseau: Father of Government Schools', paper presented at the British Educational Research Association Conference, September 1999.

Oakley, A. (1975), *Sex, Gender and Society*. London: Temple Smith.

O'Brien, L. M. and Schillaci, M. (2002), 'Why do I want to teach anyway? Utilizing autobiography in teacher education', *Teaching Education*, 13, 1, 25–40.

O'Donnell, S., Andrews, C., Brown, R. and Sargent, C. (2007), 'INCA: The international review of curriculum and assessment frameworks internet archive' *www.inca.org* (accessed 12 June 2008).

Ofsted (2004), 'Out of school: A survey of the educational support and provision for pupils not in school', *www.ofsted.gov.uk/ofsted_home/publications_and_research* (accessed 20 August 2008).

Oni, C. S. (2005), 'Comparative adult education: The nature and approaches', *Journal of Social Science*, 11, 3, 243–248.

Ord, W. (2006), 'Dear teacher, where are we going?', *www.independentthinking.co.uk/Cool+Stuff/Articles/569.aspx* (accessed 2 August 2008).

Organisation for Economic Development and Co-Operation (2006, 2007), 'Education at a glance: Highlights', *www.sourceoecd.org* (accessed 17 June 2008).

Perry, L. and McWilliam, E. (2007), 'Accountability, responsibility and school leadership', *Journal of Educational Enquiry*, 7, 1, 32–43.

Peters, R. S. (1966), *Ethics and Education* (ninth edition). Oxford: George Allen & Unwin.

Phillips, D. (2006), 'Comparative education: method', *Research in Comparative and International Education*, 1, 4, 304–320.

Piaget, J. (1985), *Equilibration of Cognitive Structures*. Chicago: University of Chicago Press.

Pimentel, C. (2006), 'The human right to education: Freedom and empowerment', *Multicultural Education*, 13, 4.

Pollard, A. (1996), *The Social World of Children's Learning: Case Studies of Pupils from Four to Seven*. London: Cassell.

Portman, N. and Weingartner, C. (1969), *Teaching As a Subversive Activity*. New York: Dell Publishing Company.

Power, C. (2006), 'Education for the future: an international perspective', *Educational Research Policy and Practice*, 5, 165–174.

Qualifications and Curriculum Authority (2008), 'The Big Picture', working draft, April–June 2008, *www.qca.org.uk/library/Assets/media/Big_Picture_2008.pdf* (accessed 2 August 2008).

Reay, D. (2004), 'Finding or losing yourself? Working-class relationships to education' in Ball, S. J. (ed.) *The Routledge Falmer Reader in Sociology of Education*. Abingdon: Routledge Falmer.

Romanowski, M. H. (2001), 'Common arguments about the strengths and limitations of home schooling', *The Clearing House*, 75, 2, 79–83.

Ranson, S. (1994), *Towards the Learning Society*. London: Cassell Education.

Raywid, M. A. (1998), 'Alternative schools: The state of the art', *Educational Leadership*, 52, 1, 26–31.

Rhamie, J. (2006), 'Eagles who soar: How African Caribbeans achieve success', paper presented at BERA, 6–9 September 2006.

Ribbens, J. (1993), 'Facts or fictions? Aspects of the use of autobiographical writing in undergraduate sociology', *Sociology*, 27, 1, 87–92.

Ridgeway, J. (2008), 'Challenge: Coping with complexity', *www.beyondcurrenthorizons.org.uk* (accessed 2 August 2008).

Riggall, A. and Sharp, C. (2008), 'The structure of primary education: England and Other Countries' in *Primary Review Research Survey 9/1*. Cambridge: University of Cambridge Faculty of Education.

Rix, R. and Twining, P. (2007), 'Exploring education systems: Towards a typology for future learning', *Educational Research*, 49, 4, 329–341.

Robinson, C. and Fielding, M. (2008), 'Children and their primary schools: Pupil's voices' in *Primary Review Research Survey 5/3*. Cambridge: University of Cambridge Faculty of Education.

Rogers, A. (2003), 'What is the difference? A new critique of adult learning and teaching', Leicester: NIACE. Cited in Smith, M. K. (1999, updated 2 July 2008) 'Learning theory', *The encyclopedia of informal education*. Available at: *www.infed.org/biblio/b-learn.htm* (accessed 20 July 2008).

Rousmaniere, K. (2000), 'From memory to curriculum', *Teaching Education*, 11, 1, 87–98.

Sadovnik, A. R. (1991), 'Contemporary perspectives on the sociology of education' in Ballantine, J. H. and Spade, J. Z. (eds) (2008) *Schools and Society: A Sociological Approach to Education* (third edition). Los Angeles: Pine Forge Press.

Sanborn, R., Santos, A., Montgomery, A. L. and Caruthers, J. B. (2005), 'Scenarios for the future of education', *The Futurist,* January–February, 27–30.

Sander, W. and Krautmann, A. C. (1995), 'Catholic schools, dropout rates and educational attainment', *Economic Inquiry*, 33, 217–233.

Sandford, R. and Facer, K. (2008), 'Futures review: Looking at previous global futures', *www.beyondcurrenthorizons. org.uk* (accessed 2 August 2008).

Schrader, C. (2004), 'The power of autobiography', *Changing English*, 11, 1, 115–124.

Schriewer, J., Orivel, F. and Swing, E. S. (2000), 'European education systems: The framework of tradition, systematic expansion and challenges for restructuring' in Swing, E. S., Schriewer, J. and Orivel, F. (eds) *Problems and Perspectives in European Education*. West Port, CT: Prager.

Schoetzau, B. (2007), 'Study says universal education is attainable and affordable', *Voice of America*, 17 January 2007. Available at *www.amacad.org/pdfs/EducationAllChildre/pdf* (accessed 3 August 2008).

Sewell, K. and Newman, S. (2006), 'What is education?' in Sharp, J., Ward, S. and Hankin, I. (eds) *Education Studies: An Issues Based Approach*. Exeter: Learning Matters.

Sextou, P. (2003), 'Theatre in education in Britain: Current practice and future potential', *NTQ*, 19, 2, 177–188.

Sharp, C., Chamberlin, C., Morrison, J. and Filmer-Sankey, C. (2007), 'Playing for success and evaluation of its long term impact', DEfS Research Brief No RB844.

Shor, I. (1992), *Empowering Education: Critical Teaching for Social Change*. Portsmouth, NH: Heinemann.

Shuayb, M. and O'Donnell, S. (2008), 'Aims and values in primary education: England and other countries' in *Primary Review Research Survey 1/2*. Cambridge: University of Cambridge Faculty of Education.

Shudak, N. J. (2006), 'The maddening road toward meaning: Questioning the word concept that is education', *Journal of Thought,* Fall, 17–22.

Smith, E. (2003), 'Failing boys and moral panics: Perspectives on the underachievement debate', *British Journal of Education Studies* 51.3 (September), 282–295.

Smith, M. K. (1999, updated 2 July 2008), 'Learning theory', *The encyclopedia of informal education, www.infed.org/ biblio/b-learn.htm* (accessed 20 July 2008).

Smith, M. K. (2004, 2005), 'Extended schooling: Some issues for informal and community education', *The encyclopedia of informal education,* www.infed.org/schooling/extended_schooling.htm (accessed 19 September 2008).

Social Exclusion Unit (1998), 'Truancy and School Exclusion: A Report' *www.socialexclusion.gov.uk* (accessed 20 May 2000).

Soysal, Y. N. and Strang, D. (1989), 'Construction of the first mass education systems in nineteenth-century Europe', *Sociology of Education*, 62, 277–288.

Spender, D. (1982), *Invisible Women: The Schooling Scandal*. London: Writers and Readers.

Standish, P. (1999), 'Education without aims' in Marples, R. *The Aims of Education*. London: Routledge.

Sternberg, R. J. (2004), 'Four alternative futures for education in the United States: It's our choice', *School Psychology Review*, 13, 1, 67–77.

Stewart, W. (2006), 'U-turn on faith schools', *Times Educational Supplement*, 8 December 2006.

Stronach, I. (2006), 'Inspection and justice: HMI in Summerhill School' in Vaughan, M. *Summerhill and A. S. Neill*. Maidenhead: OUP.

Sullivan, A. and Heath, A. F. (2002), 'State and private schools in England and Wales', Sociology Working Papers, *www.sociology.ox.ac.uk/swps/200202.html* (accessed 10 September 2008).

Tabberer, R. (1997), 'Primary education: Expectations and provision', Inca, *www.inca.org.uk* (accessed 15 July 2008).

TES (2006), 'Non-faith schools under attack', *The Times Educational Supplement*, 19 May 2006.

TES (2008), 'What the faith schools experts think', *The Times Educational Supplement*, 25 July 2008.

The Prince's Trust (2002), 'The way it is – school's out: A research summary', www.princes-trust.org.uk/Main%20 Site%20v2/about%20us/research.asp (accessed 28 August 2008).

Tomaševski, K. (2005), 'Globalizing what? Education as a human right or as a traded service', *Indiana Journal of Global Legal Studies*, 12, 1, 1–79.

Tomaševski, K. (2001), 'Free and compulsory education for all children: The gap between promise and performance', Rights to an Education Primer, no 2. Gothenburg: Novu Grafiska. Available at: *www.rights-to-education.org/content/primers/rte_02.pdf* (accessed 10 August 2008).

United Nations (1948), 'The universal declaration of human rights', *www.un.org/overview/rights/html* (accessed 20 April 2008).

United Nations Educational, Scientific and Cultural Organisation (1999), 'The four pillars of learning', *www.unesco.org/delors/fourpil.htm* (accessed 2 August 2008).

United Nations Educational, Scientific and Cultural Organisation (2008), 'Education for all global monitoring report', *www.unesco.org* (accessed 20 April 2008).

Usher, R. (1998), 'The study of the self: Education, experience and autobiography' in Erben, M. (ed.) *Biography and Education: A Reader*. London: Routledge.

Valentine, G. (2008), 'Changing spaces, changing places?', *www.beyondcurrenthorizons.org.uk* (accessed 2 August 2008).

Vanderstraeten, R. (2006), 'How is education possible? Pragmatism, communication and the social organisation of education', *British Journal of Education Studies*, 54, 2, 160–174.

Van Oteghen, S. L. (1996), 'Using oral history as a motivating tool in teaching', *JOPERD*, 67, 6, 45–48.

Vaughan, M. (2006), *Summerhill and A. S. Neill*. Maidenhead: OUP.

Vygotsky, L. S. (1978), *Mind and Society: The Development of Higher Psychological Processes*. Cambridge, MA: Harvard University Press.

Walford, G. (2003), *British Private Schools: Research on Policy and Practice*. London: Woburn Press.

Wasley, P. (2007), 'The home-schooled students rise in supply and demand', *The Chronicle of Higher Education*, 54, 7.

Willis, P. (1979), *Learning to Labour*. Aldershot: Gator.

Winch, C. (2002), 'The economic aims of education', *Journal of Philosophy of Education*, 36, 1, 101–116.

Winch, C. and Gingell, J. (1999), *Key Concepts in the Philosophy of Education*. London: Routledge.

Winch, C. and Gingell, J. (2004), *Philosophy and Educational Policy: A Critical Approach*. London: Routledge Falmer.

White, J. (1982), *The Aims of Education Restated*. London: Routledge and Kegan Paul.

White, J. (2002), 'Education, the market and the nature of personal wellbeing', *British Journal of Educational Studies* 50, 4, 442–456.

White, J. (2007), 'Towards an aims led curriculum', www.qca.org.uk/qca_6128.aspx (accessed 5 August 2008).

White, J. (2008), 'Aims as policy in English primary education' in *Primary Review Research Survey 1/1*. Cambridge: University of Cambridge Faculty of Education.

Whyte, J. (1983), *Beyond the Wendy House: Sex-Role Stereotyping in Primary Schools*. York: Longman.

Wringe, C. (1988), *Understanding Educational Aims*. London: Unwin Hyman Ltd.

Wyse, D. (2003), 'Children's Rights' in Crawford, K. (ed.) *Contemporary Issues in Education: An Introduction*. Dereham: Peter Francis Publishers.

Youth Justice Board, *www.yjb.gov.uk/en-gb* (accessed 12 August 2008).

# Index